Tales from 1978-79 Alabama Football: A Time of Champions

Steve Townsend

Sports Publishing L.L.C.
www.SportsPublishingLLC.com

Direction of production: Susan M. Moyer
Project manager: Greg Hickman
Developmental editor: Kipp Wilfong
Copy editor: Cynthia L. McNew
Dust jacket design: Kenneth J. O'Brien

ISBN: 1-58261-425-3

Printed in the United States.

SPORTS PUBLISHING L.L.C.
www.SportsPublishingLLC.com

This book, Tales from 1978-79 Alabama Football: A Time of Champions, *is dedicated to the memory of Al Browning, Aruns Callery, John Forney, Jim Goostree, Dr. H. Boyd McWhorter and Alf Van Hoose—gentlemen of extraordinary intelligence and integrity, but most importantly, they were my friends and shared these moments with me.*

Acknowledgments

Certainly this isn't the first, nor will it be the last, book to be written about Alabama football. No program in the Southeastern Conference has accomplished as much as the Crimson Tide on the playing field, and certainly the plethora of prose that has been written about the achievements of Bama football has already filled hundreds of tomes.

The vignettes included in this work could not have been written without the memories of so many who shared their stories of this special time and place at the Capstone or without the repository of information stored at the Paul W. Bryant Museum.

Ken Gaddy, curator of the museum, along with his staff of Jan Adams, Olivia Arnold, Esther Cade, Kenny Denton, Charlene Givens, Brad Green, Clem Gryska, Wayne Phillips, Gary Shores and Taylor Watson make research an experience of friendship at the Bryant Museum, and without their kindnesses, certainly most of the missing links in this book would not have connected.

Coach Gryska and his old coaching buddy Dude Hennessey traveled with me to see many of the players cited in this work.

Also, Kent Gidley, the athletic department's superb photographer, and his administrative assistant Stephanie Wooley along with sports information aides Brenda Burnette and Bryant Burnette were equally generous with their time in assisting me. I'm lucky to have them as friends.

Most of all thanks to the players and staff of the 1978-79 teams, champions all, on and off the playing field. They won with dignity and lost with class, an example taught by their mentor Paul Bryant, and a simple creed that all coaches, players and even fans should forever adopt as their own.

Contents

Prologue

As the sun descended behind ever-amassing clouds that shrouded the New Orleans skyline, the citizens and visitors to the Crescent City were already reveling on the streets, celebrating the final hours of 1978 and the birth of a new year, 1979, indifferent to the reports of an imminent and a pronounced rainstorm that was rapidly approaching from the west.

Aruns Callery, the backbone of the Sugar Bowl and a close personal friend of Coach Paul Bryant, and I entered the legendary coach's hotel suite high atop the Hyatt Regency to pay an early evening visit and to check on him one final time before Alabama's national championship showdown with Penn State the next day.

As we entered the room, the coach, outwardly relaxed but with his stomach certainly churning in anticipation of yet another football war, sat at an elegant table lined with telegrams of well-wishes, sharing a moment of camaraderie with three of his closest friends in the media, Alf Van Hoose of the *Birmingham News,* Al Browning of the *Tuscaloosa News,* and forever the "Voice of the Crimson Tide," John Forney.

Bryant's longtime security aide Billy Varner stood guard outside the suite's main entrance, and an hour or so after we had settled in chairs near the coach and his other visitors, a knock on the door signaled the arrival of the head trainer and aide-de-camp Jim Goostree, who was there to give the coach one final injury and illness update.

There were no buildings between those two high-rises back then, and the coach, his stature immense, his charisma immeasurable, rose from his seat and shuffled slowly to the dark windows, peering out at the street lights that illuminated a city on one of its biggest party nights of the year.

With glasses atop his head, an unlit pipe clenched in his teeth and knowing Goose's arrival served as a cue for us to exit, Van

With the 1:00 p.m. kickoff less than 18 hours away, Bryant stared out the window, seemingly for an interminable period of time, before answering to all of us, or none of us, maybe to all the fans wishing to know his response or perhaps just to himself.

"It'll be like all big games. Probably, come down to a big play or two in the fourth quarter, and the team that makes 'em will go home happy and the team that doesn't will always wonder what they could have done differently. I just hope and pray tomorrow Alabama makes those plays."

Chapter 1

What Happened Behind the Scenes

"I have to do what is best for the Southeastern Conference."
—Paul Bryant to SEC commissioner H. Boyd McWhorter and the Sugar Bowl's Aruns Callery

If not for Paul William Bryant's close personal friendship with New Orleans' Aruns Callery, a member of the Sugar Bowl Committee, it is questionable whether there would have been any celebrations in the Crescent City by Alabama fans after the 1979 and 1980 postseason events.

Actually, the process of uniting the SEC and the Sugar Bowl began in the spring of 1975 when Bryant informed Callery that he thought he was going to have a good team and he wanted to play a prominent opponent in the first ever Sugar Bowl in the newly built Superdome. During that time Alabama was about the only conference team that could name its annual bowl ticket, and the SEC had no contract with the Sugar, much less any other bowl.

"When Paul told you something, you didn't even need a handshake," said Callery. "I was feeling pretty good, knowing we were going to get Alabama before the season ever started in '75." Indeed, the Tide finished 10-1 and after numerous phone calls to Joe Paterno, Callery had secured the matchup Bryant had wanted back in the spring.

The 13-6 Alabama victory on December 31, 1975, would serve as a precursor of an even more titanic battle three years later. A few months after the first Sugar Bowl in the Dome, Callery approached SEC commissioner McWhorter with the idea of the SEC champion being locked into the Sugar Bowl.

"You'll never get it passed," said McWhorter. "Coach Bryant will never go for it, because he doesn't need the Sugar Bowl." And he didn't and Callery knew it, but he persisted anyway.

"When I first brought the topic up with Paul, he wasn't too keen on it," remembered Callery. "He told me that just about every year he could go to either the Cotton, Orange or Sugar, and he liked taking his teams to different spots every year."

After mulling over the idea for a few weeks, Bryant called Callery back, telling him he had reconsidered the proposal. "He said, 'Aruns, I've got to think about the rest of the conference and this is the best thing for the rest of them',' recalled Callery. "At the SEC March meeting in 1976, the league approved the recommendation at its session in Savannah, Ga."

There was one clause in the contract that almost haunted Bryant and his Crimson Tide during its championship seasons, a last-appearance rule, which coincided with the Big 10's regulation for the Rose Bowl. In both 1978 and 1979, Alabama almost lost out on Sugar Bowl invitations because of that stipulation that would ultimately be lifted after the 1979 season and cost the Tide a final Bryant appearance in the New Orleans Classic after the 1981 season, a season in which Georgia and Herschel Walker tied the Tide for first in the league. The Bulldogs, much to Callery's dismay, were offered the bid over Alabama.

January 3, 1978

Alabama players were disconsolate over the news that their 35-6 romp over Ohio State the day before, Monday, January 2, had not been enough to catapult the Crimson Tide into the No. 1 spot.

"I always thought someone else was wearing my championship ring," said safety Murray Legg, who had played a prominent role in the 11-1 season and would become an even more valuable member of the '78 team. "When we started our winter workouts on January 16, there was a determination that we wouldn't let this happen again."

Every player who went through the dreaded winter conditioning drills agreed the sweat and toil they endured under the strict guidance of Ken Donahue and Jim Goostree would serve as a lasting reminder that no matter how bad a situation may seem on the field, they would will themselves to do as Coach Bryant preached to them, "Gut check" — a euphemism for digging deep inside oneself in the most dire situation and finding a way to win.

"Let's put it this way, there was no team in better condition or mentally tougher than us," said Jeff Rouzie, a linebacker coach on the championship team and a former star linebacker for Bryant. "Other teams may have had better athletes, but none were tougher than Alabama."

"We were not always the most gifted athletically," said halfback Major Ogilvie. "But we were a team, and the team was built in the lower gym of Memorial Coliseum in the winter months. Heck, everything was easier after that."

May, 1978

ABC-TV had complete rights to all NCAA football in the 1970s, and the rule stated explicitly that a team could appear during the regular season a total of five times over a two-year period.

With a schedule featuring Nebraska, Missouri, Southern California and Washington in the non-league, the Tide was ripe for the plucking by ABC. On May 21, ABC officials finalized a deal that would move the Alabama-Nebraska game from November 18 to September 2 for a prime-time national telecast.

Already having an open date before Auburn, the switch of the Cornhusker game signaled another oddity: two open dates before the traditional season ender.

Bryant offered this spiel about the schedule: "We are pleased to open the season for TV. Certainly, as a football coach I'm not too happy with the athletic director who made up this schedule, but I'm hopeful we'll be able to compete somehow against those teams." Of course, Bryant served in a dual role as head coach and athletic director.

August, 1978

At the annual Skywriters' Tour, Jack Hairston of the *Gainesville Sun* asked Coach Bryant if he could take a moment to talk about the Alabama team before Bryant did. The coach nodded, knowing some spoof was about to occur.

Mimicking Bryant's mumbling delivery, Hairston outlined the Alabama team and closed by saying, "As you can see we aren't going to be very good and we'll probably end up going 1-10 but playing in the Sugar Bowl for the national title." Bryant joined the rounds of laughter.

In his retort, Bryant asked, "Jack, how do you know so much about my team?" With the return of such '77 luminaries as quarterback Jeff Rutledge, running back Tony Nathan, center Dwight Stephenson, and tackle Jim Bunch, the Tide offense was expected to be very good, though the loss of wide receiver Ozzie Newsome and fullback Johnny Davis left a dent in the offense, as did the loss of three starting offensive linemen: Bob Cryder, Lou Green and David Sadler.

Defensively, the Tide's losses were significant in the secondary with the departure of halfback Mike Tucker and safety Mike Kramer. Noseguard Terry Jones was on his way to the pros with Newsome, Davis and Cryder, while end Dewey Mitchell had also completed his eligibility. Despite the losses, the expectation level was feverish in Tuscaloosa.

Coach Paul Bryant with his close friend Aruns Callery of the Sugar Bowl.
(Photo courtesy of Paul Bryant Museum)

The first AP poll for the 1978 season was released in August, and Alabama was locked in the No. 1 spot followed by Arkansas, convincing winners over Oklahoma in the '78 Orange Bowl.

Keith Jackson and his ABC crew arrived in Birmingham on Thursday, August 31 to prepare for the Alabama-Nebraska game, and the self-proclaimed "Football Capital of the South" brimmed with eager anticipation of the '78 season.

Chapter 2

The Tide Shucks the Huskers

*"Walking off the field at Nebraska last year, their fans were
hollering at me pretty good, telling me to throw some more
interceptions. This game certainly erases any memories of that."*
—Jeff Rutledge after the 20-3 win over Nebraska

The Drive

It was a season that started with "the drive" and culminated
with "the goal-line stand," and if it hadn't been for that drive,
then there may have never been that stand.

Early in the second quarter of the Nebraska game and trailing 3-0 courtesy of a 48-yard field goal by Billy Todd, the Crimson Tide offense found itself literally a couple of inches from its
own goal line after punter Tim Smith's kick rolled close but not
into the end zone.

"It was a drive that pretty much signified Coach Bryant's
iron resolution to win," said offensive coordinator Mal Moore.
"Jeff Rutledge did a great job of leading us down the field, but we
won it up front, just like all games are won.

"Jim Bunch, Buddy Aydelette, Dwight Stephenson, Vince Boothe, Mike Brock and Rick Neal were the guys up there and they just knocked Nebraska off the ball."

Starting from the shadows of the north end zone, the Tide didn't race down the field; it methodically rolled up yards as well as clipped time off the clock. Before the Tide eventually scored on the second completion of the march, a 10-yard pass from Rutledge to Major Ogilvie, there was a mere 3:06 left in the second quarter. It had taken 16 plays to do it, but Alabama had completed its longest drive. Fourteen of them were running plays, including chain-moving power runs by backup fullback Billy Jackson, who picked up 14 on a third and eight from the three-yard line and then 10 on third and seven from the Tide's 20.

Tony Nathan added runs of 12, 11 and 12 before Rutledge hit Bruce Bolton for 14 to continue the Tide's roll down the field. Lou Ikner, subbing for Ogilvie, knifed through the defense for seven and six as the Tide neared the south end zone.

"We had third and goal from the four, and Major beat their defensive back [Andy Means] deep in the right corner of the end zone," said Rutledge. "He made an over-the-shoulder catch. It was a great catch."

The Redwood Forest

Alabama's "Redwood Forest Defense" intensified its pressure on quarterback Tom Sorley, and the fierce rush of Marty Lyons, Curtis McGriff, Byron Braggs, and E. J. Junior ultimately forced an interception by Don McNeal at the Cornhusker 38 in the third quarter, setting up the second touchdown drive.

An 11-yard run by Ogilvie on a third-and-10 play moved the chains at the 28. "Bruce Bolton got a great block," said Ogilvie. "I really didn't have much to do with it."

Nathan and Rutledge, old Birmingham high school rivals from Woodlawn and Banks, ripped off gains to the two, where Nathan took it in for the score. Roger Chapman's PAT failed, leaving it at 13-3 with 1:26 left in the third.

"Was I surprised at the score?" rhetorically asked linebacker Barry Krauss back to the press. "Yes, I was. I really didn't think they would score and they probably shouldn't have. After the second touchdown it was probably over with."

In an era when the radio voices of John Forney, Doug Layton and Jerry Duncan became not only synonymous with Alabama football but also served as the eyes and ears of the fans, their cries of the "Redwood Forest Defense" became a symbol of pride of the Tide. Actually, the genesis of the "Redwood Forest Defense" belongs to Charley Thornton, the former Tide associate AD and TV co-host with Coach Bryant.

"Charley started calling the 1973 [team] that had Mike Raines, John Croyle and Skip Kubelis the Redwood Forest," said Kirk McNair, the longtime SID and *Bama Magazine* editor. "Through John's broadcasts they became really well known, but it was Charley's idea."

The Cornhuskers remained ineffective the rest of the game as the "Redwood Forest" engulfed ballyhooed backs I. M. Hipp and Rick Berns, who couldn't average but three yards a carry on 26 tries for the night, and the air attack could net but 64 for the game.

After driving to the Nebraska five, the Tide fumbled it to the Huskers, a second Bama turnover deep in the adversary's territory, but this time Rickey Gilliland pounced on Sorley's fumble at the Nebraska five and two plays later Rutledge executed the coup de grace by running it in from the three with 2:17 left.

The Slip

One Alabama player who was happy with the win but not with his play was end E. J. Junior, who told Al Browning after the game, "Early in the fourth quarter I intercepted a pitchout and had nothing but green in front of me for a touchdown. I had visions of a touchdown, but I slipped and fell down."

From a coaching grade standpoint, the player who played best for the defense was sophomore free safety Ricky Tucker, who scored a 94. Offensively, fullback Steve Whitman and receiver Bruce Bolton played the perfect games, acing the night with 100s.

A Major TD

Major Ogilvie's TD reception and all-around outstanding play could not be minimized. He scored a 95 for his performance, but he suffered cartilage damage in his left knee, an ailment that would plague him the rest of the season.

"I didn't practice much the rest of the season and it was really tough playing on the turf," said the Major. "Every Friday for the rest of the year, I'd go to Dr. E. C. Brock and Coach Goostree on Friday and they would get this big needle and drain the fluid. That wasn't a whole lot of fun."

Prime Time on ABC

In an era when it was a rarity to be on television—the official rule stated a team could be on a maximum of five times in a two-year window—Alabama opened the season with Nebraska on prime time. In that particular era, before the court ruling of '83 opened the TV floodgates, Alabama had also debuted in prime time on ABC in '75 against Missouri and in '81 against LSU.

Bama Officiates Bama

There was a split crew at Legion Field that evening against Nebraska and one of the officials from the Big-8 Conference was a gentleman from Colorado by the name of Alabama Glass. His father had been from Goodwater, Ala., and his mother from Cullman, and when they moved to Colorado, they decided to take a little of Alabama with them and thus they named their son.

Redwood Forest Defense Attacks Nebraska
(Photo courtesy of The University of Alabama Archives)

The Weather Wasn't to the Bear's Liking

Before the game, Alabama's Bryant wasn't pleased about the weather. It was too nice and springlike. "We've been practicing in 100-degree weather with the humidity up there as well," Bryant told his old friend Aruns Callery at the team hotel in Bessemer. "Dang if it isn't going to be 70 degrees with no humidity just like Nebraska wants it to be."

"Paul, you worry about everything," laughed Callery at his friend's concerns.

No Tickets

In an era when a season opener at Legion Field meant zero tickets for the most nominal foes, the game against national power Nebraska meant there were zilch to be found—not in the stands and not in the press box either.

"We maxed out at 500 press passes several weeks before the game," said Kirk McNair. "We'd been turning down requests for weeks. We had media here from all over the country." After the game that Sept. 2, McNair told Jimmy Bryan of the *Birmingham News*, "I am just thankful the *New York Times* is on strike and can't be here, because we'd have nowhere to put them."

The year before when the Tide opened against Ole Miss at Legion Field, several thousand fans had barreled through an open gate to gain entry to see their crimsons play. That wasn't the case this time around, as extra security administered admissions.

Chapter 3

Tide Shows 'Em at Mizzou

"When I blocked the punt, it bounced around and I lost sight of it while I was on the ground. I felt a lot better when I saw Rickey [Gilliland] pick it up and I knew he was going to score a TD."
— E. J. Junior

A See-Saw Half

After studying Missouri films of its 3-0 season opening win over defending national champion Notre Dame, Alabama's Paul Bryant expected a down-in-the-dirt defensive fight.

"I always teach my players to expect the unexpected," said Bryant after the game. "I should heed my own advice. I didn't expect a game like this—at all."

It was a hot, windy day in Columbia, Missouri's Faurot Field, and both the heat and gusts would factor into the final 38-20 outcome. After holding Mizzou on its first series, Alabama started from its own 29-yard line with 13:34 left in the first quarter and with 11:09 left, the Tide had accomplished what Joe Montana and the Fighting Irish couldn't for an entire game: score a touchdown.

In lightning fashion, Tony Nathan carried four straight times for gains of 23, 6, 3 and 3. Then Jeff Rutledge hit Keith Pugh for 13 to move it to the Tiger 23. On the next play Major Ogilive swept down the field for the first touchdown, and Alan McElroy's field goal made it 7-0.

Using the wind to its ultimate advantage, Alabama's Woody Umphrey launched a 56-yard punt to the Tiger one with 7:55 left in the quarter, and another short Mizzou punt had the Tide back in business at the Tiger 37, where seven plays later Alabama was up 14-0 after Rutledge hit Rick Neal for a TD from the five.

With the clock winding down to end the first quarter, Missouri's terrific passing tandem of Phil Bradley and Kellen Winslow was thwarted by an interception by Murray Legg at the Tiger 28.

Alabama, with Steadman Shealy and the second team now in, marched quickly to the three, but the Tigers stiffened, forcing a short field goal by McElroy, making it 17-0.

If there was celebrating on the Tide sidelines, it was premature. Bradley led the Tigers on a 72-yard scoring drive with running backs James Wilder and Earl Gant pounding away for 10 plays. After the Tide failed to move it, Bradley kept the ball, moved behind a devastating block by Winslow and fled 69 yards for another score.

Now trailing 17-13 after missing the extra point, Missouri really took control, with Tiger Russ Calabrese intercepting a Rutledge pass and returning it for a TD and another pick ended a Bama threat late in the quarter. It was 20-17 and Bama was in trouble.

Halftime Sermon

"I don't know if I'd ever seen Coach Bryant so animated than he was at the half," said safety Legg.

"He really chewed us out and that's being polite. He went around the room and he'd point at some of the players and basically tell them you've been reading too many press clippings and not worrying about being a player or a team. Let's put it this way: he got his message across."

"It was a hot, hot day," said coach Clem Gryska. "But Coach was hotter than the weather. He had the unique ability to know what to say and when to say it. He asked them if anyone wanted to make a big play. I'd say some of them responded in the way he wanted."

"Man, was Coach Bryant livid," said linebacker coach Jeff Rouzie. "I don't know if he was madder at the players or the coaches. I know we all got the message. I don't know if I told the three who were playing the most for me [Barry Krauss, Rich Wingo and Rickey Gilliland] much, but I think they picked up the pace in the second half."

The Blocked Kick

"There is no play that can kill you like a blocked punt for a touchdown," said Paul Bryant. "I've been on both ends, and there is no doubt, the blocked punt changed the whole game."

After Alabama failed to move to start the third quarter, Missouri took over at its 26 and moved to its own 48, where it faced a third and two. Marty Lyons made one of his game-high 17 tackles, stopping the Tigers for no yards and setting up the turning point.

"We'd thought all week long that if we couldn't beat them in the kicking game, we couldn't beat them," said defensive coordinator Ken Donahue, who made the call for the block attempt.

Delivering a slam-dunk of Monte Montgomery's punt, Junior grasped for the bounding pigskin and admitted smiling and sighing when he saw Gilliland pick it up at the 35 and head toward the goal.

It wouldn't be Gilliland's only big play of the third quarter. After Alabama marched to the Tiger 42 later in the quarter, Billy Jackson fumbled on a first-down play, but on the ensuing play

Gilliland nabbed Wilder's fumble at the Tiger 40, setting up a Bama TD drive.

An end-around to Tim Clark for 25 and a pass of 12 to Jackson moved the Tide to the goal line, where Nathan scored to make it 31-20. Alabama's defensive and offensive surge continued when Curtis McGriff knocked Wilder loose from the ball at the Tiger 26 and on the first play of the fourth quarter, Rutledge went airborne on the to Ikner for another Bama TD.

With his team up 38-20, Bryant—as was his wont—played his reserves, particularly on offense, in the fourth quarter with third-string back John Turpin carrying eight times and chewing up yards and the clock.

Gilliland Player of the Week

When Rickey Gilliland picked up the Junior blocked punt, he had an unusual escort to the end zone, a black dog that had found its way to the sidelines.

"Yeah, I saw that rascal," said Gilliland to Al Browning after he was picked as the SEC Defensive Player of the Week. "He looked at me and I looked at him, and we went about our business. He chased me all the way to the bench."

During the game, Gilliland had nine tackles, recovered the fumble and caused one. As far as grades from Rouzie, he received only a 69, which was the highest of the linebackers. Marty Lyons got the highest mark for the D with his 75.

Offensively, guard Mike Brock and center Dwight Stephenson were the big winners with their 86 and 84 scores, unusually high marks for linemen. Major Ogilive played his usual superior game, netting a 90, best of the regular skilled folks.

Mike Price

Mike Price, a young assistant coach for the Missouri Tigers under Warren Powers and the tutor of gifted quarterback Phil Bradley, came away impressed with the Crimson Tide while also marveling at the skills of some of his own players.

"Phil Bradley's an extraordinarily gifted athlete who can run and throw," said Price. "With backs like Wilder and a tight end like Winslow, we felt we had the ability to strike against any defense, including Alabama's."

Bradley asked his own question to the press after the game and answered it as well, "What are the odds of lining up and beating Notre Dame and Alabama on back-to-back weekends? We felt we could. Our season is far from over, and we have some other tough games ahead of us, especially Oklahoma and Nebraska.

"I don't know if any of them are as good as Alabama. Notre Dame is strictly a physical team. Alabama's quickness is what amazes you. Their big linebacker [Barry Krauss] chased me down from behind in the second half. They all can run."

From an Alabama perspective, Marty Lyons rejected the notion the Tide had a second-quarter collapse. "I don't think we gave up 20 points in the second quarter," said Lyons. "I think Missouri earned them. They were playing at 100 percent. They are one tough team, and some others are going to find it out."

Surprise 65ᵗʰ Party

Before heading to Missouri, there was one surprise for head coach Paul Bryant, who celebrated his 65ᵗʰ birthday on the Monday before the game, September 11.

Coming off the practice field in Tuscaloosa and still dressed in a coaching shirt, Bryant headed to Birmingham with his security aide Billy Varner to speak to the Touchdown Club.

Rickey Gilliland stops Mizzou's James Wilder.
(Photo courtesy of The University of Alabama Archives)

Doug Layton, the analyst for the radio network, interrupted Dr. Gaylon McCollough, the former Tide center, who was going to introduce Bryant. "I have a little bit more business to conduct," said Layton, and with that he opened a door of Bryant allies from across the country.

"It was a special moment for all of us," said Layton. "You rarely fooled Coach Bryant, but I think we did that night."

Among those in attendance were Darrell Royal, Duffy Daugherty, Fred Russell and actor Dale Robertson, as well as a host of other former players, including Joe Namath.

"Paul, I don't know if you are the best coach in the world," said Daugherty, the retired Michigan State coach, "But you sure as hell cause the most commotion wherever you go."

"If I'd known you were going to do this, at least I'd dressed up some," quipped Bryant. "This is what I always thought my funeral would look like, with a bunch of football people."

Chapter 4

Beware of the Trojan Horse

"You can learn a lot more from losing than you can from winning, and now we'll have an opportunity. If we have character and class, and I think we do, we'll be all right."
—Paul Bryant after the 24-14 loss to Southern Cal

A year after the Crimson Tide had defeated John Robinson's No. 1 Southern California Trojans in the L.A. Coliseum, the SC coach was determined his team would avenge the defeat on Alabama soil, or in this case on the artificial surface of Birmingham's Legion Field.

Inopportune turnovers, an apparent Trojan turnover turned into a touchdown, missed scoring opportunities, poor tackling—you name it, Alabama did it, but Bryant accepted the loss as the result of his inability to prepare his team for the contest and praised the victors for being the better team.

"We didn't play with oneness and that's my fault," said Bryant from the Bama press room. "Our players just didn't have any fire in their eyes or any purpose out there today, and that's my fault, too. Southern Cal wanted it more, and Coach Robinson did a better job of getting his team ready to play.

"I didn't think we were the best team in the country coming in here today. I thought we might have a chance to the best team later in the season, but you have to improve every week and we went backwards today—and that's my fault, too."

Robinson and his offensive staff devised a plan that worked, and it was greatly aided when Wayne Hamilton, the star defensive end and a key player in the Tide win over the Trojans in '77, went out with an arm injury on the first play of the game.

The Trojan game plan was simple: quarterback Paul McDonald would go to the line of scrimmage with two plays and he would audible into a play away from where safety Ricky Tucker was lined up. When Tucker moved right, the Trojans attacked left. When Tucker inched to the left, SC struck right.

"Alabama has a very sophisticated defense," said Robinson, "and the quarterback has to make the right read. For us, McDonald did just that."

On its first drive, SC, behind an offensive line that featured Anthony Munoz, drove to the Tide one, but Murray Legg's fumble recovery stopped that scoring threat. Only seconds later, though, SC took the lead it would never relinquish. Starting from Alabama's 40, SC needed exactly one play, a 40-yard run by the eventual 1979 Heisman Trophy winner Charles White, to go up 7-0.

The Critical Second Quarter

Late in the first quarter and trailing 7-0, Bryant inserted his second team, leading to one of the most pivotal sequences of the game.

"Coach Bryant was never scared to put in the second team," said quarterback Steadman Shealy. "I'd torn my knee up in the spring and not many people thought I'd play in '78, because I had had both cartilage and ligament damage. I was back for the Missouri game and Coach put me in near the end of the first quarter."

And with good results. Starting from his own 20, Shealy directed his team 79 yards down the field, including a 33-yard burst by Lou Ikner and a 22-yard completion to Bruce Bolton.

With the ball on the Trojan eight, fullback Billy Jackson exploded to the goal line and one official ruled it a touchdown only to have his decision overturned by another. An apparent slip by Tony Nathan on fourth down resulted in a change of possession, setting up a bizarre penalty and an eight-minute SC drive.

Facing fourth and five from its 16, SC punter Marty King hit a low line drive that rolled out of bounds just inside the midfield marker, but there was a flag on the field, and Alabama was whistled for an illegal block that was ruled to have occurred before the ball was dead, thus giving the Trojans the ball back at the Tide 31. In today's world of football, there would have been no turnover and Alabama would have retained possession.

Converting three third downs and running 18 plays, SC reached the Bama 11 before settling for a Frank Jordan field goal to make it 10-0 at the half.

McNeal's Picked on His Pick

After the two teams exchanged second-half touchdowns, a 40-yard run by Major Ogilvie and a 39-yard pass from McDonald to Kevin Williams, Southern Cal led 17-7, but the game was far from over.

Facing a third and four from the Tide's 40, McDonald lofted a pass to Williams, but it seemed as if he had aimed for Bama cornerback Don McNeal, who settled under the ball at the 20.

Timing his jump, McNeal clutched the "interception" in his hands, but the cheers of the Alabama fans suddenly disintegrated into a collective moan of disbelief when the football slipped through into the arms of a racing Williams, who went in for a touchdown to make it 24-7.

"I have no excuses for not intercepting the pass," remarked McNeal. "I had it in my hands and let it slip through. It was my fault, but it was one of those games when as a team we made a thousand mistakes. I think if I had held on, then we would have still had a chance, but I didn't make the play and USC did. It couldn't happen again in a million years like that."

After getting the ball back on the kickoff, the Tide quickly went 86 yards, with Rutledge hitting tight end Bart Krout on a 41-yard TD pass, ending the scoring for the day but not some excitement.

Alabama sped back down the field to the SC 18, only to lose it on a fumble by Nathan, and after McNeal atoned for his missed interception by blocking a punt, the misery continued and ended when Rutledge's last pass was picked off in the end zone.

An Apology from the Coach

"Coach Bryant came up to me after the game and apologized for not playing me more," said quarterback Steadman Shealy. "I had played a lot against USC in the Coliseum in '77, and we knew we could effectively run the option against their defense.

"Jeff was a lot better passer than me, and I was probably a little better at running it. On this day, we probably should have run more of the true option."

The lack of energy and fire in the eyes of the players didn't go unnoticed by safety Legg either. "It was one of those games that the crowd was listless and the players' concentration wasn't what it should have been, especially considering the opponent," said Legg. "That's taking nothing away from Southern California because they had a great team, but we had already played Nebraska and Missouri, and we didn't have the zip or emotional high we had in those two games."

Longtime Bryant colleague and football maven Alf Van Hoose of the *Birmingham News* judiciously offered his opinions as well. "I used to hear all the great coaches say, 'It's not who you play, it's when you play them.' And I can assure you no one knew this better than Paul William Bryant. He was usually good at sched-

Ricky Tucker was the man SC feared.
(Photo courtesy of The University of Alabama Archives)

uling to make sure there were spaces between the bigger games, but that wasn't the case in '78 when there weren't many breathers at all.

"Coach Bryant told me, as he would say a 'zillion times,' that you really can't get a team up to a true peak but about three times a year. Simply put, SC was ready to play its A-game and Alabama wasn't, and the results were what they were."

Chapter 5

Fish or Fowl—Good or Bad

"I've got two eyes and I've been watching football for 40 years and my eyes never seen a team like this. It's fish or fowl. We're either real good or real bad."
—Paul Bryant after the 51-28 win over Vandy

A cascade of boos serenaded the Crimson Tide team as it entered its fourth quarter of the fourth game of the year, clinging to a narrow three-point advantage over perennial SEC punching bag Vanderbilt. In all honesty, Alabama was fortunate to be up 24-21, having trailed 21-16 before Tony Nathan broke free on a 63-yard TD run and caught the subsequent two-point pass from Jeff Rutledge to give Bama a field goal margin.

"When I looked up at the scoreboard and saw we were behind, I just said to myself, 'Wow,'" remarked Nathan. "I never thought about losing, but once you're behind and the way things were going I wasn't so sure. I knew I had to make something happen, and I'm glad the coaches gave me the chance."

It was an encouraging word from Bryant that assuaged the sagging football esteem of Nathan, who had fumbled twice in pivotal points of the fourth quarter against Southern Cal and then lost early against the Commodores.

"I was running to the sidelines, with my head down," said Nathan. "Coach Bryant met me, and I was worried, 'Oh me, what is he going to say?' He told me to forget about it and start playing the way he knew I could. I was more determined than ever to make him happy."

Nathan's third-quarter touchdown ignited a 27-point fourth-quarter explosion that featured a 41-yard TD pass from Jeff Rutledge to Rick Neal, a three-yard run by Rutledge, a 28-yard jaunt by Billy Jackson, and a 61-yard burst by Lou Ikner.

For the afternoon, the Tide had rushed for 448 yards, including 163 on seven carries by Nathan, and passed for 121 more, but Bryant was not happy.

"We are not as good as we were the first day we reported in August and that's because I haven't done a very good job," said Bryant. "We have to take a real hard look at what we are doing. With the games we have coming up, we'd better get some folks well and start playing better or we are in for a rough ride."

Vandy—the Rival Game

For Alabama defensive end E. J. Junior, there was one game he marked on his football calendar—and it wasn't Tennessee or Auburn; it was Vanderbilt.

"Everybody at Alabama wants to beat Tennessee and Auburn," said Junior to reporter Al Browing. "But I'd rather beat Vanderbilt than anyone else on our schedule."

A native of Nashville, Junior had been sandwiched between the Commodores and the Tide in a rare recruiting battle between those two schools. "I wanted to go to Alabama," said Junior. "I signed with Alabama and never looked back."

With an old high school teammate on the Vandy team and a couple friends cheering on the Vandy bench, Junior said it only inspired him when the Commodores took their 21-16 lead.

"There wasn't any way I was going to let Alabama lose," said Junior. "Of course, the offense pretty much took care of things without my help."

The Jeers Weren't Appreciated

The boos that rained down on Bryant-Denny Field didn't exactly elicit a favorable response from the players, as reported by Al Browning.

It didn't sit well with their teammates. "The fans really don't know what is going on most of the time," said Lou Ikner." "I just let it go in one ear and out the other."

"All I can say is they'd better be booing me and not my players," said Bryant. "Anyone who boos a college football player isn't a college football fan, and we don't need them around our program."

Marty Lyons perhaps summed it up the best: "Coach Bryant asks us to represent the school with class and dignity. Maybe some of the fans should heed his advice as well."

Freshmen Begin to Take on Additional Duties

In 1972 the NCAA passed a rule allowing freshmen to compete on the varsity level in football and basketball, but it didn't pass the legislation to allow a freshman redshirt rule until 1978, and it passed it retroactively, giving those who didn't play in '77 a redshirt year, which impacted fast-rising nose tackle Warren Lyles.

"I almost left during the '77 season when I found out I wasn't going to play," said Lyles. "I'm a football player and I want to be out there playing football, not standing on the sidelines in street clothes."

And the '78 team was beginning to have unexpected help from a few first-year players, including Lyles and true freshman safety Jim Bob Harris. Lyles had earned playing time against Southern Cal the week before and a start against the Commodores.

Jeff Rutledge fights for yardage against Vandy.
(Photo courtesy of The University of Alabama Archives)

"I felt pretty good about the way I'd played against SC," said Lyles. "It was a lot better against Vanderbilt because we won." Harris had his second interception of the year against the Commodores, and another emerging frosh, Thomas Boyd, had a sack.

In fact, Harris had played so well that he earned an 86 grade, the highest of any defender. Offensively, there had been a bunch of winners, including the quarterback tandem of Rutledge and Steadman Shealy with each scoring in the 80s. As had become a routine, the top scorer on the offensive side was Major Ogilvie, who had a team-high 95.

Shealy's Return

When Shealy had gone down with a wrecked knee in the spring, he relied on his faith and self-will to return to the football field, though no one gave him much of a chance. Matter of fact, it was unheard of for a player to recuperate so quickly from a cartilage and ligament-damaged knee.

"The good Lord did it for me," said Shealy, who rehabbed as much as six hours a day and slept with a 125-pound weight on his leg to strengthen the injured knee. "The Vandy game was my first real test because I was out on the field a lot more. The knee held up well, and I can thank God for that."

The Goal Remains the Same

Although Bryant may not have been pleased with the overall inconsistency of his team through the month of September, he still had not given up on the squad or his unquenchable thirst for winning another national title.

"We want to be national champions. That sure as hell is our goal. It might not be realistic after we play Washington, but we haven't given up on the notion quite yet.

"I might be more worried about getting out of town if we get beat."

Chapter 6

No Sleeping in Seattle

"I was lined up in my linebacker spot, trying to concentrate on the great Washington offense, and I looked out there and there was the Puget Sound. It was a surreal moment, seeing the sailboats and the Husky players all in one scene."
—Linebacker Rich Wingo

Alabama's only trip ever to Washington invigorated the spirits of the Tide, momentarily eliciting some smiles and raising the expectation level that the Tide might indeed rise back into the national title picture.

Defending Pac-10 champs and Rose Bowl victors over Michigan, Don James's Washington team was primed for the upset, if you'd call it that, because the Huskies were skilled and expecting to win.

The key to the Husky attack was fleet receiver Spider Gaines, who certainly spun a web over the Tide defense, and running back Kevin Steele. Warren Moon, star of the '78 Rose Bowl, was gone, but his replacement, Tom Porras, was no slouch.

"We wanted to control the ball as much as we could," said offensive coordinator Mal Moore. "Their passing attack was dangerous, and we knew we had to sustain our drives."

Which the Tide did, taking the opening kickoff and clipping half the time off the first-quarter timer, but the drive stalled in Husky territory, forcing a punt.

Rickey Gilliland got a fumble recovery off a bobble by Steele, too, but Bama couldn't move it, forcing a 50-yard punt by Umphrey that bounded into the end zone, setting up the first big play of the day.

"Gaines was something else," said linebacker coach Jeff Rouzie. "He could just flat-out run, and he ran right past our defense." A 74-yard pass from Porros to Gaines gave Washington a 7-0 first quarter lead.

The Tide Answers Back

Tony Nathan almost returned the favor on one play, taking the kickoff and almost breaking it the distance before being tripped up at the Bama 48. Nine plays later, Major Ogilvie was skirting the right side for 13 yards and a touchdown. Washington made it 10-7 when Mike Lansford hit a 37-yard field goal with 2:46 left in the half.

Trailing by the same score with 7:44 left in the third quarter, E. J. Junior, a master of the big play, made a huge one, blocking a punt and setting the Tide up at the 16-yard line. The four-play drive was simple power football: Nathan for four, Billy Jackson for five, Ogilvie for six, and Nathan for the final one. McElroy's PAT sailed wide right, and the Tide clung to a 13-10 lead.

Frantic Fourth

Washington appeared poised to take the advantage back when Nathan fumbled a punt on his own 30 with 11:58 left in the game, but Marty Lyons and Curtis McGriff clogged up the middle on first down and Lyons chased down Steele for a gain of four on second down. On third and four from the 24, Steele tried Gary DeNiro's side and was thrown back for a two-yard loss. Lansford's attempt to tie it was wide left and short as well.

It took the Tide 1:13 to make it 20-10 with Ogilive gaining 22 and Rutledge eight more, setting the stage for a 36-yard TD pass from Rutledge to a wide open tight end Rick Neal.

"One of the beauties of the wishbone is the ability to pass off it," said coordinator Mal Moore. "Washington was reeling from our option, and Rick just ran free and Jeff hit for the score. It was a huge play, and thankfully, it was enough for us."

Quarterback Rutledge called it this way. "I noticed that they were cheating to one side of the field on the play before, so I thought Rick could get open in the middle. I wanted to throw the ball earlier, but I had to dodge a rusher. When I looked up, Rick was all alone, no one within 10 yards of him on the goal line."

The TD was barely enough for Bama to hold on. For the second time Gaines raced past the Tide secondary and nabbed a scoring pass from Porros, this time from 58 yards out, and with 5:50 left in the game it was back to a three-point contest.

Efficiently, Alabama rambled back down the field, moving to the Husky 26, but a fourth-down pass failed, thanks to a botched officiating call. Alabama was ruled for pass interference, which not only gave the ball to Washington but after a 15-yard assessment put it on the 41-yard line. Porros fired away, and a fourth and 12 interference call on Wingo gave the Huskies a first on the Bama 36, but Murray Legg cinched it by recovering a Steele fumble.

Back on Track

Alabama players felt the team was back on track and gaining momentum again. Linebacker Wingo, who had seven tackles, said as much after the game. "I think we played one of our better defensive games of the year. We had a great week of practice. I had a knee strain against Nebraska and had not been effective. We are not a great defense, but if we keep working hard and improving we have a chance to be pretty good."

Marty Lyons, who had 12 tackles, was as much relieved as happy, "We put a lot of hard work and prayers into this game. Today, the work paid off and the prayers were answered. This game will make us a much closer team."

And, Murray Legg called it this way, "Today, we got a big, big win—for ourselves, for Coach Bryant and for our state."

Where Did DeNiro Come From?

"Have you come down to earth yet?" Barry Krauss quizzed defensive end Gary DeNiro after the win. The question was a good one, because the sophomore end, starting for the injured Wayne Hamilton, put on a dazzling show, making 10 tackles, including four for losses totaling 16 yards?"

"I just have to keep improving," said DeNiro, deflecting the sudden attention for his outstanding play.

TV at Memorial Coliseum

More than 7,000 fans paid for the right to watch the game at Coleman Coliseum, and the crowd was becoming somewhat filled with angst when there was no picture. Finally, as kickoff neared and the pregame show trashed, the video flickered and the fans cheered. It wasn't the first ever pay-per-view for an Alabama game, though. Actually, that happened in 1948, the renewal game with Auburn, when 2,000 fans crammed into the armory near Legion Field and heard John Forney call the action. Paul Bryant's aide Charley Thornton was serving as the play-by-play man from Seattle.

While 7,000 watched it on the big screen at Memorial, 4,000 Alabama fans flew across the country to see the matchup with

Steve Whitman plows ahead against Washington.
(Photo courtesy of The University of Alabama Archives)

the Pac-10 power. "We could have easily sold 10,000 tickets," said Kirk McNair, the sports information director. "That's all we got and we sold."

Quick Trip to Canada

Head coach Paul Bryant had been late for the Friday afternoon press conference the day prior to the game and he quipped it was Charley Thornton's fault. "I got in the car and Charley took off," said Bryant. "We kept driving and driving. I said, 'Charley, I think we are in Canada.' I don't know if we were or not, but I know it is cool up here. I'd rather play in Tuscaloosa where it's near a 100 degrees than up here in this 60-degree weather."

Bryant confidante and *Tuscaloosa News* sports editor Al Browning said, "Coach that doesn't have anything to do with you beating them 52-0 in '75 and all their players passing out in the warm-ups due to the heat."

"Not at all," quipped Bryant.

Chapter 7

The Bear Was A-Growlin'

*"I bet those Tennessee folks are sitting up there licking
their chops getting ready for us. If I were the Alabama
people, I'd be looking at the football coaching situation.
Our people are probably doing that right now. The worst part
of our coaching today was the head coaching. This is the
poorest-coached team we have had around here."*
—Paul Bryant

Doug Dickey, once considered the coach most likely to sup-
plant Paul Bryant as the "man" in the SEC, brought his final
Florida team to Tuscaloosa on a sunny 60-degree October afternoon, and judging from Bryant's disappointment, one would have
deemed Dickey had won the ultimate round against his old spar-
ring mate.

Bizarre Start

If Bryant was growling, Dickey was chomping away as well,
disconsolate over the loss and at a loss for words about the coin

toss that impacted the first quarter. There was a 12 to 15-mile-an-hour wind blowing from the south, and Dickey instructed his team he wanted to go on defense first. There was no deferring in '78, so captain Don Swafford told the ref he wanted to kick and Alabama suddenly had the ball and the wind.

Yet the Tide didn't take an immediate advantage of the faux pas, as the first drive resulted in a failed field goal try by Alan McElroy and the Gators jumped ahead 3-0 on a 34-yard field goal by Berj Yepremian, the younger brother of the Miami Dolphin star and Super Bowl goat.

"I didn't know what happened on the kickoff," said Dickey. "I thought Alabama had won the toss and then I saw what happened. I wasn't too happy. As it happened, it was the worst of both worlds for us."

Dickey got even more ticked later in the first quarter as Alabama scored on the final play of the quarter. Taking advantage of the wind, Jeff Rutledge went airborne, hitting Keith Pugh for 16. Facing third and five, the Tide tried a halfback pass, but Major Ogilvie's toss was incomplete. A penalty on the Tide, a procedure, nullified the play, allowing Ogilvie to try yet another pass, and this one worked, a 14-yard completion to Rick Neal.

A play later Rutledge rifled a 20-yard pass to Bruce Bolton and Rutledge took it in from the 13 to make it 7-3.

As swiftly as the wind was whirling around Bryant-Denny Stadium, the momentum of the game changed just as quickly in the second quarter, with the Tide clinging to a 7-3 lead and the Gators threatening from the Bama nine.

The star of the Florida team was a quarterback turned wide receiver by the name of Cris Collinsworth, who was a lightning rod with the ball under his arm and the national leader in kickoff returns, and he had visions of a touchdown dancing in his head when he circled end after taking a pitch from quarterback Tim Groves.

Alabama defensive end Gary DeNiro, starting for the injured Wayne Hamilton, had a different idea, though, as he battered Collinsworth, forcing the football to bounce on the artificial surface. Curtis McGriff recovered for Alabama, and three plays later Billy Jackson took a handoff from Jeff Rutledge and bolted 87 yards for a touchdown, ultimately the longest of the year for the Tide, and Alabama never looked back, though it never really pulled away, either, winning 23-12.

After Jackson's long-distance run, Florida wrested momentum away in the second quarter, when Yepremian sailed through a 52-yard field goal and the Gators fielded a short punt on its 38. Groves broke containment to get it to the 21 with :38 left in the half, but Murray Legg's interception at the goal line helped the Tide to escape more damage.

Finally a Win

The third quarter was equally nightmarish for Bryant, as his team lost a fumble and punted twice for an average of 22 yards, but the defense did its deal by holding the Gators to a mere first down. Finally, the offense rolled downfield, but the frustrations continued when Bama bogged down on the 15 and had to settle for a 32-yard field goal by McElroy.

Yet the game tightened quickly, as Florida used a trick play, an end-around pass from Tony Stephens to John Smith that covered 38 yards and set up a 19-yard pass from QB John Brantley to Stephens to cut the lead to 17-12.

Alabama did stop the two-point conversion as Brantley's pass to Collinsworth fell incomplete.

Tony Nathan's 52-yard kickoff return was nullified by a clip, pushing the Tide back to its own 10, and the Gators were inspired, but not for long.

"Entering the game, we felt like we could throw the football on Florida," said receiver Pugh in the postgame interviews. "We felt Florida didn't have much confidence in their secondary. I believe our passing game is coming along. We don't have an Ozzie Newsome this year, and maybe us receivers need a little more confidence."

Indeed, on the first play, Rutledge launched a 40-yard pass that Pugh deftly and acrobatically caught in the style of Newsome between Gator defenders Warren Gaffney and Juan Collins.

A 16-yard pass to Neal and some pounding by Billy Jackson and Nathan took the Tide to the Gator 16, but it was fourth and two, and Bryant had to make a decision with 7:26 left in the game.

"We felt like we needed a touchdown to win the game," said offensive coordinator Mal Moore. "The worst scenario was Florida would be backed up deep in its own territory. We had moved the ball fairly effectively, but we just hadn't scored, and really Florida hadn't done much offensively the whole game."

Facing the critical fourth, Rutledge performed one of his best fakes ever, drawing the defense to fullback Jackson, and the Tide senior hit the left side for seven yards and a first to the nine. A play later Nathan bowled over two defenders to score the final points of the game. A two-point pass from Rutledge to Nathan was no good.

Collinsworth Depressed

Collinsworth along with Dickey were the most disconsolate Gators, with the future TV announcer Collinsworth murmuring to the media, "Hopefully, this won't affect me in the future, but it is going to affect the hell out of this weekend. We came in here thinking we could win. I fumbled the ball on the four-yard line and gave them the lift they needed. Alabama has a good team. LSU and them are probably the two best teams that we have played."

Dickey simply said, "The key to the game was the run by the fullback. That really stunk."

Nathan Fan Club

Tony Nathan and his Alabama offense, though not high on Coach Bryant's charts that day, evoked praise to the press from Gator linebacker Scot Brantley, who finished with a game-high 16 tackles: "Alabama has a great disciplined team. They have a lot of players that I respect highly. Tony Nathan is a great back. I think he is as good as Charles Alexander. When LSU plays Alabama, it is going to be some kind of game."

"We want to be a championship team," acknowledged Nathan. "But it's hard to tell right now. It's time for us to decide how much winning means to us. I'll be surprised if we don't get turned around and start playing better."

Bryant Continues to Growl

Perhaps Bryant was using one of his psychological ploys to get his team focused on Tennessee, but the Bear's rant continued well after the game, as he continued to lament where his team was headed to the press corps. "Can we still be a great team?" Paul Bryant asked after the game. "It can't if we keep doing the same mistakes we are making. Great teams don't make the mistakes we make. Maybe I'm thinking it means more to our players than it actually does.

"Nobody gets penalties or fumbles it around intentionally, so it must be the coaching. To be honest, we looked like a pickup team that plays every Sunday afternoon. I'm sure we had some individuals who played well, but as a team we didn't show much.

"Our kicking game was pitiful. Our kickoff coverage and returns were the only good things about it.

"I don't think we are 75 percent as good as we were when we played Nebraska.

"We were very fortunate to get out of this thing alive. Florida came to play and they were well prepared for us."

Billy Jackson's 87-yard TD run vs. the Gators.
(Photo courtesy of The University of Alabama Archives)

DeNiro's Day

Despite Coach Bryant's overall displeasure, he had to be content with the play of Gary DeNiro, who finished the day with 10 tackles with an amazing six for losses for a minus 20, and he caused two fumbles. His play didn't go unnoticed in the SEC either, as he was picked as the conference's Defensive Player of the Week for his play against the Gators.

And other than the kicking game and fumbles, the Tide did control the Gators, with a 23-8 edge in first downs, 306-75 in rushing, 190-119 in passing, and 496-194 in total offense.

Chapter 8

The Tennessee Waltz and Other Victory Dances

"To me beating Auburn is the thing, but to Coach Bryant it's beating Tennessee. They don't dance around when we beat Auburn, but they sure do when we beat Tennessee."
—Tony Nathan

There was no doubt that the Tennessee game intensified the enthusiasm in both camps, and the perilous trip to Knoxville would be the turning point—one way or the other for the 1978 season.

On the Wednesday before the game, the following quote from the Volunteers' second-year coach John Majors appeared on the door leading to the Alabama dressing room:

"I would like everybody in this great country of ours, blacks and whites, Arabs and Jews, Swiss and Polish, French and German, Protestants and Catholics to join all together and beat the hell out of Alabama!"

Scrawled across the message was a simple one-line admonition from Jim Goostree: "DON'T LET IT HAPPEN!!!"

An overflow crowd of 85,436 jammed into venerable Neyland Stadium, but most clad in orange had long gone before the Vols scored a pair of late fourth-quarter TDs to make the final score 30-17, misleading though respectable.

Actually, it was the Volunteers who proved hospitable hosts when Robert Malone fumbled a Woody Umphrey punt at the six-yard line late in the first quarter and versatile Lou Ikner recovered at the six.

On third and four, the Tide's Mal Moore pulled a trick out of his offensive bag, a tight end option to Tim Travis. "We put the play in for Tennessee, feeling it could be effective and catch them somewhat off-guard," said Moore. "Jeff [Rutledge] did a great job of reading the defense and pitching it to Tim and getting us the lead."

The Second Team Rolls

Paul Bryant was never scared to put his second unit in, at any point or anywhere on the field. With the Tide clinging to its 7-0 lead and backed up on its own nine, the Bama legend inserted his second-team offense and challenged them to hold on to the ball.

"Coach Bryant had the unique ability to understand people and understand situations," said backup quarterback Steadman Shealy. "He had confidence in us, and therefore it transferred to us. We always wanted to prove to him that we could do the job and repay that confidence."

In a 15-play, 90-yard drive, executed to perfection, the Tide wishbone never passed, unless you count passing the goal line, to score its second TD of the day. Shealy did the honors, keeping in the option on a third and five from the Big Orange 15. The extra-point snap was errant, and holder Kevin Jones's attempt at running it in was stopped, leaving it at 13-0 Tide.

Amazingly, that was the only time the Tide touched the ball in the quarter as the Volunteers kept the ball the remaining 19 plays of the half, moving to the Bama 10 before settling for an Alan Duncan field goal.

The Third-Quarter Dominance

Although Alabama proclaimed the fourth quarter was theirs, on this blue-skied autumn day high in Rocky Top, it was the third quarter, as the Tide scored 17 and misfired from the Vol 22, or it would have been worse.

After McElroy kicked a season-best 41-yard field goal to make it 16-3, Barry Krauss recovered a Frank Foxx fumble at the Vol 13. Rutledge ran for eight before adeptly reading the defense and feeding fullback Steve Whitman for the final five to make it 23-3.

The last TD was set up by another turnover, an interception by Jim Bob Harris, who returned it to the Tennessee 27. With the ball resting on the nine, Moore again called for the tight end option run, and after bobbling Rutledge's pitch, Travis watched the ball bounce right back into his hands, and he raced in for the final Bama TD.

About the only dramatics left were the boos that cascaded down from the orange crowd with quarterback Jimmy Streater being the recipient of the fans' ire. His backup David Rudder did come in and complete 11 of 12 passes, though for the most part they were meaningless.

Let the Dancing Begin

"Coach Bryant's pace would pick up a step or two the week of the Tennessee game," said Jim Goostree, the team trainer in a day and time when the position served as the role of administrator, coach, recruiter as well as healer. "I'd gone to Tennessee and been there under General [Robert] Neyland, so I can truthfully say I was around two of the best that were ever in this business.

"If beating Tennessee was important to Coach Bryant, it was even more important to me and Ken Donahue who had played for General Neyland. Someone once asked me if I still had any orange blood in me. I told them they could just cut me open and see how that crimson blood looks, because they sure weren't going to see any orange."

Goostree led the dancing, as he did after all the wins over Tennessee, telling Al Browning, "It was a quick version of the UT fast-step. You couldn't very well call it the Tennessee waltz because it was too fast and the music wasn't right. This was the most excited I'd ever been going to Knoxville. Before we left Tuscaloosa, I had the feeling this team was ready to make its run and it usually starts with Tennessee. There were times when I came up here that I wasn't so confident, but that wasn't the case this time around.

"I spent five years at Tennessee, and no game means more to me to win than this one."

The Players Sing

Barry Krauss, Byron Braggs, E. J. Junior, Don McNeal and Rich Wingo, defensive stars of the day, did their own little skit, taking it from the hit movie of the year *Animal House*. The quintet gathered around and sang to any who dared to listen, "Shout, take it a little higher. Shout, take it a little higher."

"We were having a blast," said Braggs, the giant defensive lineman who regaled in every win over Tennessee and astutely understood the history of Alabama football. "Rich would do this routine called the 'dead bug.' I yelled, 'Rich, it's time for the dead bug. He responded by rolling over on his back and frantically kicking his legs and arms. Just like a dead bug. Man, that was a time we had."

Byron Braggs did some dancing after the UT game.
(Photo courtesy of The University of Alabama Archives)

The Victory Cigars

"Coach Bryant brought the cigar celebration with him when he came to Alabama," said Goostree. "I'd always have them packed, but Coach gave them out to every player who wanted one."

Wingo, a co-captain for the Tennessee game, like all his teammates listened when the coach spoke. "He was standing there telling us how proud he was of all of us for winning when he pulled out a stogie and said it was time to smoke a cigar," said Wingo. "That happens every time we beat Tennessee."

The Challenges Ahead

The win over Tennessee indeed would be a turning point, as noted by a pair of players who lived the moments and spoke to the *Birmingham News'* Alf Van Hoose after the game.

"I think the pressure is off now," said Murray Legg. "The man who should receive all the credit for this is Coach Bryant. He works harder than anyone in our program, and it is time for us to work a little harder for him. The man deserves all we have to give, because he has stayed by us through thick and thin this season. He has been an inspiration."

Early-season injuries had been a factor in some of the Tide's defensive problems, particularly to end Wayne Hamilton, who suffered an arm injury early against Southern California: "This is the third time I've been able to play Tennessee and beat them all three times. There isn't anything like it. I must have been excited because I wasn't aware of my elbow hurting the least bit. I'm just happy to be able to contribute to this team again."

Interesting Viewpoints

Tennessee head coach Johnny Majors believed in the tradition of the Third Saturday in October game between the Tide and the Vols, having played in it and coached it. A friend as well as an admirer of Bryant, Majors came away even more impressed with the Alabama wishbone, telling the media, "Alabama executes the wishbone better than any team I've ever seen, and I was in the Big 8 when Oklahoma was running it. They do so much off the bone and can hurt you in so many ways. Last week against Florida, they did it with the pass. Today, they caught us on the tight end run. It is a most difficult offense to defend, and I only see Alabama getting better as this year goes on. You might have seen the national champ out there today."

Before exiting Neyland Stadium, Goostree made one final provocative and prophetic remark to Browning, "This rivalry is not going to cool down. It will just get hotter and hotter."

Back Up to No. 3

The victory over the Volunteers not only extended the Bama win streak to eight over the Vols, but it catapulted Bama back to No. 3 in the nation. Oklahoma remained atop the polls as No. 1 followed by equally undefeated Penn State. Trailing Alabama and still in the national title hunt were Nebraska, Maryland and Southern Cal.

Chapter 9

Homecoming Memories

"Goose egg, baby. Goose egg. We finally got the goose egg."
—Defensive tackle Marty Lyons

Jim Nabors, a native of Sylacauga, Ala., who had retired as Gomer Pyle of TV fame and moved to Honolulu, returned to the Capstone in 1978 to serve as the Homecoming Grand Marshal when the Tide hosted Virginia Tech at Bryant-Denny Stadium.

The theme of the '78 Homecoming, the final home game of the season at Bryant-Denny, was "In the Mood." Harriet Troxell was the Homecoming Queen in 1978 and was crowned by George Wallace.

11-Play Goal-Line Stand

Perhaps, it was an omen, but some two months before Alabama's legendary goal-line stop against Penn State in the 1979 Sugar Bowl, the '78 team had an amazing 11-play drive against Virginia Tech.

During this improbable sequence in the third quarter, quarterback David Lamie had three passes intercepted, had four more passes fall helplessly to the turf, fumbled twice and was roughed by the defense twice. Perhaps it was the unlucky No. 13 Lamie wore, or a harbinger of an even more significant goal-line stand, but Alabama's defense scored its only shutout of the year with the defensive stop in the third quarter of an otherwise easy 35-0 victory.

Here is the improbable sequence of plays that occurred late in the third quarter with Bama up 21-0 and Tech first and goal at the four.

(1) Lamie tries to run and is stopped by Marty Lyons for no gain, but Tech is penalized back to the nine for illegal procedure.

(2) E. J. Junior sacks Lamie for a loss of 10 back to the 19.

(3) Lamie drops back to pass and is hit by Warren Lyles and fumbles, but Tech guard Gary Smith picks up the loose ball and is dropped by Lyons back at the 30.

(4) On third and goal from the 30, Lamie throws down the field and Don McNeal intercepts at the two, but Tech retains possession when Lyons is assessed a personal foul for roughing the quarterback, making it third and 15 from the 15.

(5) Lamie escapes the pressure of Lyons and Junior but is nailed by Barry Krauss for a gain of two to the 13.

(6) Facing fourth and goal from the 13, Lamie's pass in the end zone is no good and Bama takes over at the 13, but one play later the defense is back on the field after Billy Jackson fumbles at the 11 and Tech's Chris Albritton recovers.

(7) Lamie throws in the end zone, but McNeal bats it down.

(8) Murray Legg blitzes and clobbers Lamie, but he forces the pass anyway, only to have Big Byron Braggs swat it down.

(9) After a delay penalty moves it back to the 16, Lamie is rushed hard by Wayne Hamilton, forcing another incompletion.

(10) Lamie throws in the end zone and Allen Crumbley intercepts it and brings it back to the 30, but Junior is called for roughing, giving the ball back to Tech.

(11) Instant replay time. Lamie throws in the end zone again and Crumbly intercepts again, bringing it back to his own 44, officially ending Tech's scoring threat.

One More Chance

Virginia Tech actually had one more attempt at scoring with :40 left when it was perched on the Bama nine-yard line, but Curtis McGriff knocked down running back Mike Romagnoli to ensure the first shutout of the year and prompt Coach Bryant, attired in a cherry sports jacket and green pants on this Homecoming day, to note, "I didn't think we would ever get another shutout at Alabama, but I hoped and prayed we would."

The Reactions Afterwards

For quarterback Lamie, who was battered and bruised on the unusual stand, he lauded his foe: "Alabama has nothing but class acts on this team. They are as good a team and as classy a team as we've ever played. The Alabama players didn't talk trash on the field. They just went about their business. They keep their mouths shut and just play hard and play to win."

Alabama players added their own perspective on the official quotes passed out after the game:

"We just reached down inside and found some way to stop VPI from scoring," E. J. Junior said. "When we get in situations like that, we just try to pretend our opponent is on our one-yard line. We checked ourselves and pulled up something important. Coach Bryant calls it a gut check. A good crowd usually helps, but you usually throw noises out of your mind and concentrate on beating the man in front of you."

"When I got my first interception, I said this was my big chance," said Crumbley "But that one was taken away. When I saw that second interception coming my way, it was the biggest thrill of my career."

Keith Pugh's pass-catching earned VPI's respect.
(Photo courtesy of The University of Alabama Archives)

Balance of the Bone

While the wishbone was a dominant running attack, no team executed it like Alabama. As legendary announcer John Forney so aptly described, "Alabama added wings to the wishbone."

In the win over Virginia Tech, Alabama rushed for 211 yards and passed for 233 on a seven-of-nine for 160-yard performance by Jeff Rutledge and a four-of-five for 73 day for his backup Steadman Shealy. Keith Pugh had five catches for 148 yards, prompting Tech safety Gary Smith to say, "Keith Pugh has the best hands of any receiver I've seen since I've been playing football. He just made some sensational catches."

Chapter 10

The Shotgun vs. the Wishbone

"Mississippi State must have thrown 100 passes today. They must have gained a mile passing out there. My gosh, the game must have lasted four hours. It seems like we've been playing since 10:00 a.m. At my age, I almost needed a nap."
—Paul "Bear" Bryant

After securing the proverbial goose egg against Virginia Tech, the Tide prepared for a Mississippi State team coming off wins over Florida State and Tennessee, and the Dawgs surprised the Tide by coming out in a shotgun and actually throwing 53 times, including 46 by starter Dave Marler, who amassed 429 yards and a TD, but the Tide offset his pass-happy performance by intercepting him four times, and Alabama rolled to a 35-14 victory.

Former Alabama player and assistant coach Jimmy Sharpe was the offensive coordinator for the Bulldogs that day and devised the sneak attack on his old team. In actuality, the Tide wasn't totally caught off guard.

"Coach Bryant always had a period during practice to work on what if they do this or if they do that," remembered secondary coach Bill Oliver. "We weren't surprised State used the shotgun like they did. We just didn't expect them to pass on every down. Coach Bryant said to us afterward, 'I don't think you can win this way. You might win occasionally, but you won't win any championships.'"

Tucker Time

Ricky Tucker, who picked off two of Marler's passes (Allen Crumbley and E. J. Junior got one each), admitted after the game to a group of reporters in the Legion Field locker room that he was exhausted and had seen all of the shotgun he'd ever want to see. "It looked like State had everybody going out for passes. I know one thing I don't want to see: the shotgun. We were huffing and puffing at the end, but as many passes as State threw, I think we played fairly well."

Besides his two interceptions, Tucker had a fumble recovery and seven tackles in helping the Tide to improve to 8-1.

Touchdown Tony

While State was flinging the ball 53 times and attempting only 16 rushes, Alabama's Touchdown Tony Nathan led an offensive rushing parade with 145 of the net of 331 yards, including an 82-yard TD run in the second quarter. "That felt pretty good, real good. If I had had to go 83 to score, I think I would have been pulled down on the one. Luckily, I had enough to get across the goal line."

Nathan also scored a clinching TD on a six-yard pass from Jeff Rutledge in the third quarter that made it 28-14, and when State drove to the Bama one on the ensuing series, the shotgun fired blanks and in essence ended all Bulldog dreams of an upset in Birmingham.

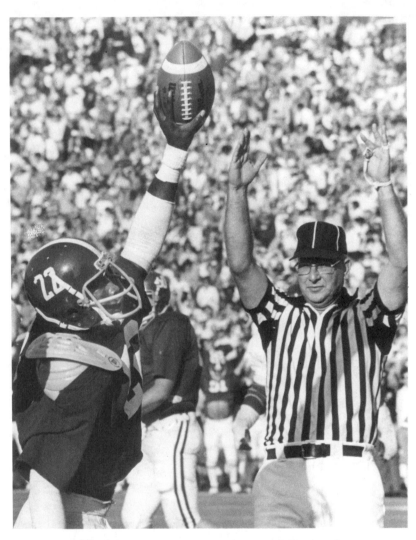

Tony Nathan hands the ball to umpire Pete Williams after a TD.
(Photo courtesy of The University of Alabama Archives)

Bama's Own Surprise

While the Bulldogs had a surprise for the Tide with its shotgun, Alabama pulled a couple of tricks of their own. "We opened in the I-formation with Tony Nathan behind Steve Whitman," said Mal Moore, then the offensive coordinator. "We ran pretty well against them, and we used the 'whoopee pass' a couple of times for big gains.

"We lined Keith Pugh in a tight end formation and Jeff [Rutledge] just flipped it to him and we got some pretty good yards out of it."

For the first time in the '78 season, MSU yielded a touchdown in the first quarter, and Bama did it twice, both on one-yard dives by Major Ogilvie, and Alan McElroy's pair of PATs gave the Tide a 14-0 lead it wouldn't relinquish.

And Coach Bryant duly noted the importance of the first-quarter success, "We thought it was important to jump on them quickly. We've beaten State a lot over the years, and down inside, we thought they might not have a lot of confidence against us."

Chapter 11

The Day Alexander the Great Met Krauss Again and Again

"Who do I compare Alabama to? Maybe the Dallas Cowboys or the Minnesota Vikings. They were super. They are big and amazingly quick. Most linebackers go parallel to the action. Alabama's just blast across the line of scrimmage."
—LSU running back Hokie Gajan

In the first showdown for the trip to the Sugar Bowl, Paul Bryant's Tide defense shut down LSU's Heisman Trophy candidate Charles Alexander, holding him to 46 yards on 13 carries, as the Crimson Tide rolled to a 31-10 victory at Legion Field.

Yet PA announcer Simpson Pepper's reading of a final score from Lincoln, Neb., Nebraska 17, Oklahoma 14 created the most pronounced stir among the denizens in crimson that November afternoon. With No. 1 Oklahoma losing, an already motivated Alabama team's spirits were elevated to an even higher level.

"We were really intense already, but when we heard that No. 1 had lost, we knew it was possible things were going to fall in place for us," said linebacker Barry Krauss. "Of course, we knew we had to take care of business against a great LSU team that featured Charlie Alexander."

The once-beaten Tigers led early, but Bama rallied for a 14-10 halftime lead before completly dominating the second half en route to its 21-point victory.

Actually, Krauss and Alexander had become friends off the field at the annual Playboy All-American gathering, but on this day that is where the friendship terminated.

After the game, the amity resumed, though, with Alexander noting, "I met Barry in Chicago and we became friends. I met him a few more times this afternoon. He wasn't as friendly. He is an All-American linebacker for sure.

"I don't think Alabama did anything special to stop me. They're just a great team. They are the most physical team we've played and they're so quick."

Despite Alexander's worst game, Krauss said, "I thought Charles Alexander was one of the best backs in the nation coming into this game and nothing has changed my mind."

TV Time

Alabama's third and final appearance during the regular season on ABC, all games at Legion Field, resulted in Krauss being selected as the TV Defensive Scholarship winner and Major Ogilvie reaping the honor for the offensive side.

Flag Day

Yellow flags littered the green Astroturf of Legion Field this November 11 with Alabama being whistled for 106 yards and LSU 91. Two critical penalties by LSU shifted the entire momentum, as a clip nullified a 79-yard TD return of an interception by Chris Williams that had apparently made it 13-0 Tigers.

Then the Bengals had a dozen on the field that negated a field goal in the second quarter.

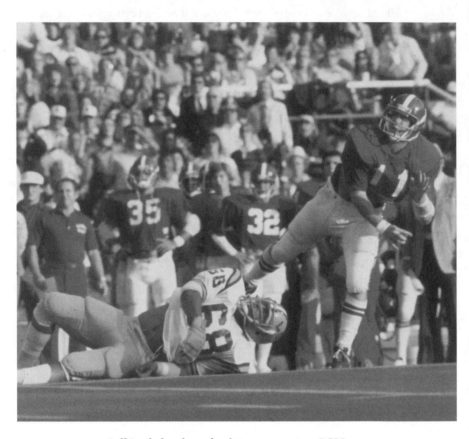

Jeff Rutledge drops back to pass against LSU.
(Photo courtesy of The University of Alabama Archives)

Besides LSU botching the field goal by having too many Tigers on the field, Alabama took advantage of the kicking game in two other opportunistic times. Punter Woody Umphrey faked a fourth and two and lofted a 19-yard pass to Lou Ikner to set up a TD run by Steadman Shealy, and Ikner recovered Williams's muffed punt at the Bengal two to set up an Ogilvie TD dive.

The Fourth Quarter is Bama's

An 87-yard drive in seven plays, which featured a 52-yard pass from Jeff Rutledge to Keith Pugh, highlighted a dagger-to-the-heart sequence in the final quarter that epitomized Bryant's clarion call of "The Fourth Quarter is Ours."

While there was some jubilation in the Tide dressing room, Alabama's quest for the Sugar Bowl dimmed with the score from Jacksonville: Georgia 24, Florida 22.

"It's obvious we're in a much better position now than we were before today," Henry Bodenheimer of the Sugar Bowl told the press. "We want an Alabama-Penn State match up, but Georgia will have a lot to say about that and Georgia will be a prohibitive favorite to beat Auburn next week and earn the Sugar bid."

Chapter 12

Bowls and Polls

"We are not where we want to be, but we have three weeks to get there. I thought we were the better team. All I'm worried about is winning the conference championship and the national championship. I'm not worried about bowls yet."
—Paul Bryant

Facing the three-week layoff before the Auburn game, the news from the bowls and the polls were not good for the Crimson Tide when they were made public November 14.

The new top 10 had Penn State perched atop the list, but Nebraska jumped over the Tide into the second slot, momentarily setting up an Orange Bowl match for No. 1 with the Nittany Lions expected to meet Nebraska. Oklahoma had dropped to No. 4 followed by Southern Cal.

"That voting business is bad news for us," said back Tony Nathan. "It seems every time votes are cast, we get voted out. I certainly don't want us to get into another situation like last year."

With Georgia having the edge on the Sugar Bowl due to the "last team to attend rule," the picture wasn't too bright for the

Tide to play on January 1 much less compete for the national title.

Houston had clinched the Cotton Bowl as the Southwest Conference Champs and Notre Dame was penciled in as the visiting team, leaving the Tide in a perplexing situation.

Alabama would need a lot of help come November 18 from Auburn against Georgia and from Missouri against Nebraska.

Krauss Player of the Week

After his 12 tackles and one caused fumble against LSU, Alabama did receive some good midweek news when Barry Krauss was voted the AP Player of the Week.

Being the team jester, Krauss was at first serious then quipped, upon hearing the news, "Individual honors don't mean much to me. I'm proud, but I'm more proud of the way our defense played. We showed a lot of improvement against LSU. It was our best game of the year. Besides I won the ABC award at the Liberty Bowl in 1976, and they never did send me that La-Z-Boy rocker they promised."

Saturday, November 18, 1978

The first of consecutive open dates found Bryant milling around his house. Fidgeting with the radio, he listened to the afternoon contest between Georgia and Auburn.

He also flipped through the TV to catch the scores, especially Penn State vs. N.C. State and Nebraska vs. Missouri. Since Alabama had played both the Cornhuskers and the Mizzou Tigers, he knew how gifted both teams were and even told one of his aides de camps, Jim Goostree, on the Friday before that he thought Missouri might upset them. "He didn't have the same confidence that Auburn could upset a talented Georgia team that had lost only to South Carolina in a non-league game," said Goose.

Barry Krauss earned SEC honors.
(Photo courtesy of The University of Alabama Archives)

"He was uncanny, though and he basically called what was going to happen with Missouri."

Miracles did happen. With its gifted running back trio of Joe Cribbs, James Brooks and William Andrews, Auburn ran wild on Georgia, though the game ended in a 22-22 tie. The blemish on Georgia's record elevated Alabama to the lone spot atop the SEC, but the Tide still had to beat Auburn to get the Sugar nod.

Even more importantly was the news out of Columbia. Missouri had indeed upset the entire bowl cart with its win over Nebraska.

Monday, November 20, 1978

The polls came out, and Alabama had rolled back again to the No. 2 spot behind Penn State, a less-than-impressive 20-9 winner over North Carolina State.

While the bowl picture wasn't as muddled, it certainly wasn't totally clear either. Paterno still liked the notion of playing in Miami, and Alabama's path to New Orleans, while now open, certainly wasn't quite paved there either. The Tide still had a must-win game against Auburn, and it was no gimme either. All Bryant had to do was refer his team to what the Tigers did to Georgia.

Bryant announced late that Monday that the seniors had indeed voted to accept a Bluebonnet Bowl trip to play Stanford and its fast-rising coach Bill Walsh if Bama lost to or tied Auburn. He was also lobbying hard to ensure the opponent would be No. 1 Penn State.

Emergence of a DB

During Alabama's layoff, secondary coach Bill Oliver found some unexpected relief for some help with his secondary with the sudden emergence of sophomore halfback Mike Clements.

"It is strange what you remember about a team," said Oliver. "The one thing that stands out to me about the '78 team was the evolution of Mike Clements as a defensive back. I had recruited him out of Erwin High School in Birmingham. I think Georgia had shown some interest, but that was about it.

"My son Brad, who was toddling around, went with me to one of his games. I was about to leave when I saw him take a kickoff and just jet by the defenders. I came back and told Coach Bryant we ought to offer him, because he could run.

"Well, after two years at Alabama, Mike really hadn't progressed much, and I didn't know whether he'd ever help us, other than being a good specialty team player. We gave the players a few days off during the layoff before Auburn and then we started practicing.

"It was like a light bulb went off in Mike's head. I'd never seen anything like it in my coaching career. The Thursday before the Auburn game I was meeting with Coach Bryant about our playing rotation.

"I said, 'Coach, you aren't going to believe this, but dang if I'm not sure if Mike Clements isn't our best defensive back right now.' Coach just nodded and said, 'I've been watching it from the tower, and in my 40 years of coaching I've never seen a player make this much progress in such a short period of time.'

"We knew we'd need Mike for the next two years, but more importantly we felt he'd help us against Auburn and, if we had the chance, against Penn State in the Sugar Bowl."

Chapter 13

Turning Iron into Sugar

*"I know not many folks gave us much of a
chance after the Southern Cal game, but I
didn't give up and the players didn't give up."*
—Paul Bryant, about the win over Auburn

There was a day and time when Birmingham's Legion Field,
painted a dark green, lived up to its sobriquet of "The Football
Capital of the South." It came alive on Saturdays in the autumn
back then, especially when Alabama rolled into town to play
Auburn on a battleground matching the intensity of a football
Civil War. Auburn liked to call it the Iron Bowl, though it was a
term Bryant didn't exactly cater to. He was more interested in
postseason bowls.

The stakes are always high when the two collide, and the
emotions more often than not run amok with the fans more so
than the players, but this December 2 contest meant everything
to both sides. A win for Alabama would pave a sugary path to
New Orleans for a national title showdown with Penn State; while
a Tiger victory would not only eliminate that dream for the Tide
but give Auburn a 7-3-1 season and reestablish it as a legitimate
SEC force.

Billy Jackson finds an opening in the Auburn defense.
(Photo courtesy of the University of Alabama Archives)

Deep into the second quarter, the Auburn half of Legion Field was electrified with excitement, and for just reasons. Coming off their tie with Georgia the previous Saturday and hopes high, the Tigers had created a ripple in the Tide and enhanced their hopes of souring the Sugar Express.

After using a fake field goal to set up a touchdown in the first quarter to off set a Jeff Rutledge-to-Bruce Bolton TD pass, the Tigers had taken a 13-10 lead when they converted a fumble into a 48-yard scoring drive, culminating in a nine-yard run by Joe Cribbs, who teamed with William Andrews and James Brooks to give the Tigers a most formidable backfield.

With the scoreboard clock reading 1:07 left in the half and starting from its own 20, Auburn coach Doug Barfield had decided to run out the clock and take the lead into the dressing room.

In his Alabama career, Barry Krauss had the unique propensity to make, as Coach Bryant would say, "the big play." A head-on collision with Andrews left both players sprawled out and searching for a bouncing, loose ball that deftly rolled into the hands of safety Murray Legg.

The energy of the split crowd shifted quickly, and Rutledge went airborne to Bruce Bolton from the 17 to give Alabama a lead it would never relinquish. Like most prototypical Bryant games, the Tide dominated the second half en route to its 34-16 win.

Leading now 17-13, Alabama's wishbone controlled the second half, starting with a 41-yard run by Major Ogilvie on the first play of the third quarter, as he blasted through the Tiger defense behind blocks by center Dwight Stephenson, left guard Mike Brock and left tackle Buddy Aydelette.

Rutledge threw a TD pass to tight end Rick Neal, and after the two teams exchanged field goals by Jorge Portella and Alan McElroy, the Tide rolled it up with a 67-yard fourth-quarter drive with Steadman Shealy scoring from the 20.

A Career Reflection

"I grew up dreaming about playing for Alabama," said safety Murray Legg. "My granddad had taken me to the Orange Bowl when Joe Namath had scored the TD that the officials didn't give him against Texas.

"I had sat in Legion Field and Denny Stadium dreaming about playing for Alabama and knowing what pride there was in wearing the crimson jersey. I'd come to Alabama to be a champion and I had paid the price. It is hard to describe it, but I remember as a freshman walking under that old tunnel that led to the practice field and seeing those guys in the red jerseys [the first team] and knowing one day I wanted to be there.

"I remember after my freshman year I was playing quarterback and I'd gotten a little down on myself. My dad had been a high school coach and he reminded me of the principle of hard work. I just worked as hard as I could.

"Before my sophomore year, I was checking the depth chart at quarterback and I wasn't even listed as the eighth-stringer. I looked over at safety and saw where I was first team and my heart leapt.

"I heard this voice behind me and it was Coach [Bill] Oliver, and I'll never forget him saying, 'Hey, old buddy, that shows what can happen when you work hard.'

"All of our seniors had worked hard and we had come close to winning the national title before, and we knew we had one more chance, against Penn State in the Sugar Bowl."

The Postgame Remarks

The two locker rooms at Legion Field lie adjacent to each other in the north end zone, and while the players were interviewed in the cramped quarters, Paul Bryant lumbered slowly to a makeshift room designated for media interviews. "I appreciate all you guys coming by," Bryant told the press. "I thought for a while that there wouldn't be anybody in here. We were really banged up coming into the game and we are really banged up coming out of it. I know we got better as the game went along. I think we have a chance at the national championship if we beat Penn State and you sports writers vote for us. I'll say this: no one has beaten Penn State this year."

Rutledge Record

When Jeff Rutledge came out of Banks High in Birmingham, there was no questioning his ability to throw a football, and the Auburn game was a high point in his career, as he completed 13 of 21 for 174 yards and the three TDs, giving him 30 for his career and 13 for the season, breaking Joe Namath's school record for career TD passes and tying Rutledge with Namath and Harry Gilmer for the single-season mark.

Like his teammates, Rutledge was more interested in what lay ahead than what had occurred. "I knew I had set the record and I feel good about it, but what was important was winning the game and having a chance for the national title. I'd rather win a game any day than set a record.

"We felt like we could throw on Auburn because they were so geared up to stop the run."

One player who took advantage of the Auburn pass defense was tight end Rick Neal, another Birmingham Banks product who caught five passes for 67 yards on the day. "They never adjusted and I was wide open most of the game," said Neal. "It was the most passes I ever caught in a college game." Entering the game, he had 12 catches for the year and 20 for his career.

Actually, the Tide was just as effective on the ground and in the air, rushing for 253 yards and passing for the 174. Major Ogilive had 104 yards on only nine carries while Shealy netted 60 on four tries.

Lyons of a Day

Marty Lyons, picked as a member of the all-time Alabama football team, had many a dominant day for the Tide D, but none any better than his performance against Auburn when he was credited with 16 tackles, three for losses, and a fumble recovery.

"It was the most important game of my career," said Lyons. "Our seniors had worked so hard for four years to get to this point. All I could think was, 'Oh yes, the Sugar Bowl.'"

With Lyons leading the way, Alabama limited Auburn to 233 yards in offense, with Cribbs getting 118 yards on 32 carries. Brooks and Andrews combined for a mere 32 on 10 attempts.

Chapter 14

The Days Leading Up to the Sugar Bowl

After Alabama rallied from a late second-quarter 13-10 deficit to beat a spirited Auburn team 34-16, much to the relief and delight of the Sugar Bowl envoys, especially Bryant's close personal friend Aruns Callery, the Tide coach and his bowl buddy sought a private moment to solidify the showdown with Penn State.

The friendship between the two had dated back to Bryant's days at Kentucky when the Wildcats scored an improbable 13-7 victory over No. 1 Oklahoma in the 1951 Sugar Bowl and had blossomed over the years. Working as friends, the two had put together the 1973 classic with Notre Dame and the 1975 battle with Penn State.

Callery worked feverishly in lobbying Paterno to forget the Orange Bowl allure and play Alabama. After the Tide victory over the Tigers, Paterno didn't need much more persuading. He eagerly accepted the challenge, living up to his pledge of wanting to play the highest-ranked opponent.

Bryant Casts His Ballot and Talks Football

Paul Bryant wasn't hesitant to note that he voted for Jeff Rutledge for SEC Player of the Year, but the Tide quarterback didn't win. Georgia running back Willie McClendon did. When asked why he voted for Rutledge, Bryant said, "Because he won the championship and has won the most games of any player in the running."

A few days after the Auburn win, while preparing his team for the Sugar Bowl, Bryant took a few moments' respite with John Forney to talk about his favorite subject: football, and the impact it had on his life.

"I believe that a football player who comes here and stays for four years is going to be better prepared to take his place in society and better prepared for life because I think he'll learn some lessons that are very difficult to teach in the home, even the church or the classroom. I think that by learning those lessons he'll win.

"He'll be a better person all the years of his life, which in my opinion, includes his spiritual, mental and physical well being. If it weren't for what I learned, I wouldn't be coaching today. You have to learn some tough lessons in life, and the quickest place to learn it, in my opinion, is a football field."

The 1978 team had learned them well, but the biggest game of their career still loomed a few weeks ahead.

December 7, 1978

Most of the All-American teams had been released, and no fewer than six Penn State players had been so honored, including the stellar defensive tackle tandem of Matt Millen and Bruce Clark. Safety Pete Harris, younger brother of NFL star Franco, rounded out the defensive picks for the Nittany Lions.

Offensively, guard Keith Dorney and quarterback Chuck Fusina were consensus picks, as was kicker Matt Bahr.

"Anyone who thinks Penn State doesn't have a bunch of great football players doesn't know much about football," said Bryant while in New York for the Football Foundation and Hall of Fame dinner. "Of course, we got some pretty good plow hands, too."

Among them were Alabama's All-American defenders, tackle Marty Lyons and linebacker Barry Krauss.

Besides Krauss and Lyons, guard Mike Brock, tackle Jim Bunch, defensive ends Wayne Hamilton and E. J. Junior, safety Murray Legg and center Dwight Stephenson had earned first-team All-SEC honors. Left half Tony Nathan and quarterback Jeff Rutledge had been named to the second units.

Paterno had begun his laborious task of watching Alabama on tape as well, and he became convinced of one thing: "I didn't think Alabama was the best team we could have played until I watched them on film," said Paterno. "I was wrong. This is by far the best team we have played or could play."

Among the players over whom Paterno marveled was center Dwight Stephenson. "He's not an All-American?" Paterno mused.

Monday, December 18, 1978

ABC-TV spokesman Don Bernstein confirmed there had been frank discussions with the Sugar Bowl and the football rules committee to allow an overtime if the game ended in a tie.

"The rumor is founded," said Bernstein from his New York office. "This game could be so close that it would be a shame for it to end in a tie. We would love to set a precedent."

Tuesday, December 19, 1978

Sugar Bowl president Robert Fabacher announced there would be no overtime or sudden death in case of a tie.

The football rules committee announced it would be on their agenda for its January meeting, though a spokesman for the group said he didn't think it would pass.

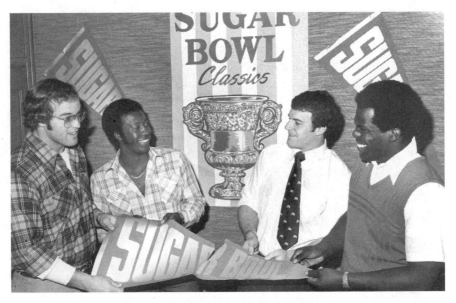

*Marty Lyons and Tony Nathan at a photo-op
with Penn State's Joe Lally and Eric Cunningham.
(Photo courtesy of The University of Alabama Archives)*

Friday, December 29, 1978

The mutual admiration between Bryant and Paterno was obvious at the press conference at the New Orleans Hyatt.

Dressed in a red sweater, Bryant said, "All I can say is Joe's the best coach in college football." When asked if that included him, Bryant said, "Yes."

Paterno was effusive in his praises of the Tide. "The last wishbone team we played was Alabama in 1975, but I really don't consider Alabama a pure wishbone team like an Oklahoma. They do so much more out of the wishbone with their offensive package.

"And defensively, they are just sound, so well coached. They just don't beat themselves."

That night in the Alabama hospitality suite atop the Hyatt, several assistant coaches including Mal Moore, Bobby Marks, Dee Powell, Jack Rutledge, Bill Oliver, and Jeff Rouzie settled in front of the TV to watch Clemson play Ohio State in the Gator Bowl.

The coaches were keenly interested because Danny Ford was making his debut as a head coach, taking over for Charley Pell who had accepted the head job at Florida for the fired Doug Dickey, a voter in the coaches' poll for UPI.

Like all football fans, the Tide staff was stunned when renowned Buckeye coach Woody Hayes punched Clemson linebacker Charlie Bauman after a late interception. Waiting for the replay to confirm what everyone thought they'd just seen, Rouzie said what everyone was thinking, "He hit him."

Indeed he had, and momentarily the upcoming Monday battle with Penn State seemed secondary.

Saturday, December 30, 1978

In previous bowl trips, Alabama's foes had remained aloof at joint team parties, but there was an instant bond between the Crimson Tide and Nittany Lion players. "I was sitting at a table with David Hannah and a couple of other players," said Murray Legg.

"Coach Paterno was on the dance floor with his wife and they came over to talk to us.

"He asked, 'Aren't you David Hannah?' and David said, 'Yes sir.' Coach Paterno then proceeded to tell us he was an old man and his wife liked to dance and asked David if he'd dance with her.

"Coach Paterno sat down with us and talked about a number of subjects, but not a lot about the game. The Penn State players and our players got together and we spent a lot of time together that night. It was totally different from my previous bowl experiences against UCLA and Ohio State."

All was not totally well for the Tide, as several players, including Major Ogilvie, came down with a stomach virus that would keep quite a few of the Crimson players up for the night.

"They had served this lavish meal of shrimp and oysters and some of us got really sick," said the Major. "Coach Goostree spent a lot of time administering medicine to us and getting us ready for the game. It wasn't the most opportune time to get sick."

Sunday, December 31, 1978

Nursing an infected ear and sipping a hot cup of coffee in his hotel suite, Bryant met with the writers who regularly covered Alabama.

"I'm proud of this team," said Bryant. "We've had a lot of injuries and we haven't done much on rushing the passer all year. We've been hurt by the pass, and Penn State can really throw the ball. I doubt if we can stop them, but I hope we can slow them down to make a game of it.

"Ricky Tucker [starting safety] won't play and E. J. Junior (end) probably won't be able to play much. Rich Wingo hasn't played much at all this year. We're pretty banged up, but that's just part of it [not citing the virus that had infected his team]. We'll patch together a team and hopefully we'll play well."

Paterno, resting in his room, beamed with confidence, particularly because of a decided edge in the kicking game.

"I think if we hold Alabama to 14, we'll win," said Paterno. "I really believe we can get 17 on them, and with a kicker like Matt Bahr, it certainly helps our chances."

Walking through the hotel lobby before the team's final curfew, affable Barry Krauss was cornered by a few media types, seeking once last quote. "I can taste it," said Krauss, licking his lips. "We've come so far since the Southern Cal loss. This is why I came to Alabama, to play for the national title."

Chapter 15

A Game for the Ages

*"It was a game for the ages. It was a game that
actually lived up to all the hype and hoopla that
surrounded it. It's a game I was fortunate to witness."*
—Keith Jackson

Monday, January 1, 1979

A torrential rainstorm deluged the Crescent City, steadily
dropping the temperatures as well. Anyone wishing for an outside venue to play the game either had to be a duck or a nut,
quipped an unknown solider in crimson as the team boarded the
buses for a short trek across Poydras Street to the Superdome.

Despite the harsh weather conditions outside, there were no
tickets to be found in New Orleans, as the dome overfilled with
crimson-and-blue-clad fans.

One banner hung over the loge area poetically claimed:

Bama is red,

Penn is blue,

Bear is No. 1,

Joe is No. 2.

With the kickoff set just for a few minutes past one, the revelers still celebrating the awakening of a New Year had little time to rest for the game of the ages.

First Half

Utilizing a blitz package designed by defensive coordinator Ken Donahue, Alabama completely dominated for 28-plus minutes, but the scoreboard didn't reflect it. It was 0-0 when Alabama took over on its own 20 with 1:32 left in the second quarter.

Penn State's No. 1-rated defense, yielding but 54 yards a game rushing and just over 200 total a game, had been instructed by Paterno to call timeouts, so that the Lions might get one last shot at scoring before half.

On first down, Major Ogilvie got three. Timeout Penn State. On second down, Tony Nathan grabbed a short pass from Jeff Rutledge. Five yards. Another Penn State timeout.

Rutledge fed it to fullback Steve Whitman on third down and the junior fullback pounded for five and a first at the 33, temporarily stopping the clock.

Following the blocks of Whitman and Ogilvie, Nathan exploded to the right for 30 yards and a first at Penn State's 37. Suddenly and spectacularly, Alabama was within scoring range. Another Nathan run netted seven more, prompting Bryant to scream for a timeout.

Bryant and coordinator Moore conferred with Rutledge and decided to take a shot in the end zone. Perfectly placing the ball in the seam, Rutledge lasered it to Bruce Bolton for a touchdown and Alan McElroy's PAT gave Alabama a 7-0 halftime lead. Penn State had only 19 yards offense in the entire half.

State Strikes Back

In the third quarter, All-American Harris pilfered a Rutledge pass and stepped to the Tide 48, setting up a tying touchdown. A 21-yard swing pass from Fusina to Mike Guman preceded a 17-yard TD pass from Fusina to Scott Fitzkee for the six.

Momentum distinctly attired itself in blue and white, and the Lions' No. 1 defense stiffened, shutting down the wishbone. But Alabama's momentary lapse defensively didn't last long. Safety Murray Legg blitzed and sacked Fusina, forcing a punt to Little Lou Ikner, a senior who had played sparingly.

"I had been back there and had fair caught four punts," said Ogilvie. "I guess Coach Bryant wanted somebody back there, at that point, who might could break a long run."

"It just shows how dumb I am," Bryant would later say after the fateful return by Ikner. "I should have had him back there the entire time."

Breaking free, Ikner raced behind a convoy of blockers, especially huge lineman Byron Braggs. The Lions finally caged Little Lou on the 10-yard line.

Overcoming an off-sides penalty, the Tide faced a third and goal from the 10, and Mal Moore called for the option left, the identical play Alabama had used to beat Penn State 13-6 in '75. All-American Millen blasted Rutledge moments before he pitched to Ogilvie who scampered down the left sideline and forced his way past the pylon for the go-ahead touchdown.

"I don't remember much about the play," remembered Ogilvie. "I do remember how good Millen and Clark were, and in the wishbone, you have to be able to do something with the tackles. We didn't have much success. Fortunately, we did on this play."

The dramatics were far from over.

The Goal-Line Stand

An errant pitch from Rutledge to Nathan in the fourth quarter set the Lions up at the Tide 19 with 7:57 left in the game, setting up the sequence of plays Paul Bryant knew would occur sooner or later. On first down, a Matt Suhey 11-yard burst up the middle had it first and goal at the eight, and only a saving tackle by Murray Legg and Jim Bob Harris averted what could have been a touchdown.

First and goal from the eight, Mike Guman headed left on a pitch only to be met on a hard tackle by Rickey Gilliland, who slammed the Penn State back down hard on the six.

On second and goal, Fusina found Fitzkee wide open for what appeared a cinch and tying touchdown.

"I always felt we were the most prepared team and I'd studied film after film of Penn State," said Legg. "In the formation they were in, I knew they were going to run a crossing route with Fitzkee and I hand-signaled Don McNeal. I had this illusion of intercepting the pass and running 100 yards and being the hero of the game.

"As I was going into coverage, I tripped over E. J. Junior and I thought for sure he was going to score and then I saw Don [McNeal] come out of nowhere and knock him out of bounds inches from the goal line."

"I knew I was a yard out of the end zone," said Fitzkee. "I was going to turn and dive in. I don't know where the Alabama defensive back came from."

"It was one of the greatest individual efforts I've ever seen," said McNeal's secondary coach, Bill Oliver. "I mean ever."

With the ball resting inches from the goal, Fusina called the bread and butter plays of the Penn State offense. First he torpedoed Suhey into the line, but the Tide front led by Rich Wingo blockaded the goal line. If there was any gain, it couldn't have been more than an inch. Fusina called time out.

Amazingly, Wingo inserted himself into the game when Gilliland limped off, holding a sore shoulder. "I really think it

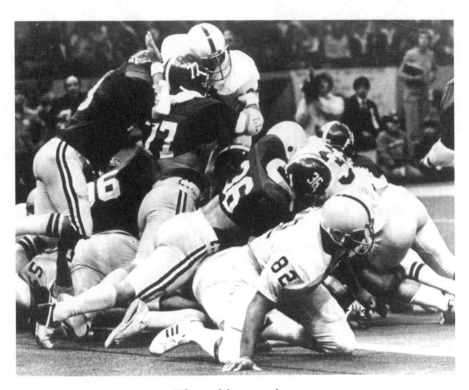

The goal-line stand.
(Photo courtesy of the University of Alabama Archives)

was an act from above," said Wingo. "I had been hurt most of the year and I just wanted to get into the game so badly. I didn't think I'd ever play pro football and this was my last chance.

"When I saw Rickey coming off the field, I just grabbed my helmet and went in there. I never gave Coach [Jeff] Rouzie a chance to put anyone else in there."

Then it was fourth down and a momentary pause in the action.

"I heard someone yelling, 'Gut check, gut check,'" said Braggs.

"I think it was Murray Legg. There was an excitement in the huddle. We were talking about this is Alabama football. This is what all what Coach Bryant had taught us. The one moment we'd worked for and sweated for, coming down to one play. It was all those winter days in the lower gym."

With his team huddled, Fusina walked up to the goal line, surveyed the lay of the land, seeing just how far they had to go. "You'd better pass," defensive lineman Marty Lyons told him. Momentarily, their eyes locked.

This time it was Guman, a big back at 212, hurtling toward the goal line, where a sea of red met him. It was Krauss who delivered the knockout blow, though it was the Tide's No. 77 who didn't initially get up for the lick. "It was a violent collision and I actually broke my helmet," said Krauss. "I had a pinched nerve, so when I hit him, my whole left side went numb. I was in pain. Marty [Lyons] leaned over me while Coach Goostree was working on me and I asked him if we'd stopped them. When he said, 'Yes,' it was the first moment I knew we had."

The Final Minutes

Yet there were more fireworks to follow. A short punt by Woody Umphrey seemed to refuel the Lions' fire, but a flag fluttered to the artificial turf. One Penn State player had forgotten to check out on the punt return unit, leaving PSU with 12 men on the field. Alabama had escaped a dangerous field position snafu.

Penn State's final effort ended when Mike Clements picked off Fusina's pass and raced it to within the shadows of the goal line.

Several assistant coaches, feeling Alabama needed to win convincingly to cinch the No. 1 spot over Southern Cal or Oklahoma, pleaded with Bryant to try for another score.

He didn't. With the clock in the Superdome signaling the time of day at 4:00, the Sugar Bowl War had ended with Alabama winning 14-7.

Postgame

UPI writer Dave Moffit asked Bryant repeatedly if he thought Alabama could have stopped Penn State on the goal line, and what were the odds of them doing it? Miffed, Bryant said, "I don't bet on football."

Finally, the coach gruffly remarked, "I bet there's only one team in the country that could have stopped Penn State and that team is Alabama.

"I think in any really big game, there are five or six plays on offense and defense; the team that makes them is the one that's going to win the game. Krauss's play was certainly a big one, but he'd never had the chance if Don McNeal hadn't made the third-down play, or if David Hannah hadn't made a great play on third down. The way it turned out, there were three great plays down there and we made all of them."

When asked what he was thinking during the series of plays, Bryant remarked, "Oh, I don't know what I was thinking. You get into a game and get tied up in it and you don't have time to feel. You hope of course that you'll stop them. I'd hope they'd fumble or I'd hope they'd do anything to keep the ball out of the end zone. As for my feeling, I was scared to death they'd get it in. I was thinking about what we were going to do on offense if they did."

Bryant wasn't the only one feeling poorly. Battered and bruised by Penn State and still ailing from the effects of the stomach virus that had spread through many members of the team, Ogilvie asked the coach if he could ride to Birmingham with his parents and miss the January 2 flight home to Tuscaloosa. "It was the most physical game I'd ever played in, period," remembers Ogilvie.

Assistant coach Jeff Rouzie, who had played in physical games and coached in many more, agreed.

"It was the most physical game I was ever involved in, as a player or a coach or a spectator. It is still the best Penn State I've ever seen, including the ones that won national championships."

ABC announcer Keith Jackson likened it to war: "In all my years of covering college football, I've never seen a more fiercely fought game than the 1979 Sugar Bowl between No. 1 Penn State and No. 2 Alabama. It was like hand-to-hand combat, a battle of gladiators who embodied the mental and physical toughness of their respective coaches, Paul Bryant and Joe Paterno."

January 2, 1979

Alabama arrived back in Tuscaloosa eagerly awaiting the results of the poll game, which in past years had often been unkind to the Tide. The results of the coaches' poll had a demoralizing impact on the Tuscaloosa campus. Southern Cal, controversial winners over Michigan in the Rose Bowl, had jumped from No. 3 to No. 1.

Both the Tide and Trojans had 15 first-place votes, meaning someone didn't vote. Enterprising journalist Alf Van Hoose of the *Birmingham News* investigated and found the non-voter was Doug Dickey, recently fired at Florida.

Another, Jim Young, the head coach at Purdue and whose offensive line coach at the time was a future UA AD Bob Bockrath, voted the Tide fifth.

Wednesday, January 3, 1979

The Associated Press, with a 38-19 first-place differential in favor of Alabama, voted the Tide No. 1. Assistant coach Rouzie was driving toward the office when he heard the news. "The AP poll in just one minute," remembered Rouzie. "Then there was this long wait between commercials. It seemed an eternity. Then they finally said, Alabama is No. 1."

Assistant coach Sylvester Croom heard the news at Bryant Hall and joked with some writers, "This proves writers aren't as dumb as we thought, and you are smarter than a lot of coaches we know."

Sports information director Kirk McNair called Bryant in his office to let him know the good news. The old warrior, papers strewn across his desk, was mapping out plans for the 1979 season and another run for No. 1.

Friday, January 5, 1979

ABC's Jim Spence had been working to put together a one-game playoff between Alabama and Southern California for the undisputed national title. "A one-game playoff seems a natural," said Spence. "We think the attention it would draw nationwide would catapult college football to a level it's never seen."

NCAA official Dave Cawood issued a terse one-sentence statement citing a bylaw that prohibits teams from competing in more than one postseason game. The proposal was shelved for another time and place.

Chapter 16

Before the '79 Kickoff

"Before his knee injury, he was quicker than a hiccup."
—Paul Bryant on Steadman Shealy

With many of the stars of the '78 team graduated, including Rutledge, Nathan, Bolton and Neal on offense, there was plenty of optimism for the offense, especially with the continued healing of quarterback Shealy. With the entire offensive line back plus starting running back Ogilvie and fullback Whitman, the offensive forecast was bright.

"When Steadman was a sophomore, I thought he'd be the most productive wishbone quarterback ever," said Bryant during the spring. "I don't think he's as sharp now. He was so quick, I said then he was quicker than a hiccup. I think, or at least I hope, he'll be fine this season."

Defensively, there were some concerns, particularly replacing the three linebackers, Krauss, Wingo and Gilliland, plus All-American tackle Lyons, All-Conference safety Legg, and cornerback Crumbley.

As matter of fact, the coach experimented with E. J. Junior at safety throughout the spring. "He's done really well," said Bryant. "But he's too far away from the action and we need him where the action is."

The Final Contract

A few weeks before the season opener, August 29, 1979, Coach Bryant signed his final contract, a five-year deal that would allow him to coach through the 1983 season. "I might retire before then," Bryant announced. "I'm not going to challenge the state's mandatory retirement law [which was 70 years]."

Although details of the final contract were never released, the whispers around the department had it that the coach/athletic director had been raised from $70,000 a year to $100,000 to help him with his state retirement. That included his perks, including his TV show, the hottest such production in the country.

It was also time for reflection for Bryant. He had gone to a reunion of his Junction Boys from Texas A&M late that spring. A quarter-century later the book about the camp would become a bestseller as well as an ESPN movie, though one who was there, Gene Stallings, admittedly is no fan of either the book or the movie. "I'll just say that they portrayed what really happened and Coach Bryant in an exaggerated manner." Stallings, always the most obliging person around for autograph seekers, refuses to sign his name on the book, even though he wrote the opening to it.

The Skywriters

When the Skywriters Tour hit Tuscaloosa, Bryant was in a most convivial mood, perhaps sensing exactly how good his current team was going to be, though he deflected the attention in his typical style.

He regaled the group with his inability to pronounce some of the names of his players through the years, including Eddie Versprille, Ray Abbruzzese, Pete Jilleba and David Gerasmichuck. "I just got rid of 'Big Chunk' a few years ago," said Bryant, "and I now I have another one." The new one was Bob Cayavec, who the coach pronounced Kaveeck.

Murray Legg and E. J. Junior display the AP Trophy.
(Photo courtesy of the University of Alabama Archives)

"I might not can pronounce it," said Bryant. "But I know this, he will knock your block off."

During the visit of the writers from around the Southeast, Shealy was optimistic about his knee being sound for an entire season. "My knee always gives me trouble," said Shealy. "I took some of the best shots I've ever taken in the spring, especially from Wayne Hamilton. As far as getting hit, there is no difference if you had knee surgery or not. Sure, it gets tired and sore during two-a-days, but all of us get tired around here during two-a-days."

Chapter 17

The Tide Wrecks Tech

"That touchdown on the last play of the game really hurt. We were planning on eating goose eggs for breakfast on Sunday when I saw those yellow and white pompons and heard the Ramblin' Wreck song."

—Byron Braggs after Alabama's 30-6 win to open the '79 season

For the first time since 1964 Alabama returned to a friendlier and safer Grant Field in Atlanta, Georgia. The last time Paul Bryant had stepped on the surface of the Georgia Tech campus he had to borrow a football helmet to walk across the field, avoiding the whiskey bottles aimed at his noggin. Of course by '79, the Tech fan base had eroded as well, and of the 57,000-plus at the game, it was estimated 30,000 of them were clad in crimson.

Time had erased much of the feud that existed between the two schools, and the once-powerful Yellow Jackets had lost most of their sting when they abruptly pulled out of the Southeastern Conference and went their own merry way as an independent in 1964.

Despite his misgivings about what had transpired between the two schools in the early 1960s, when writer Furman Bisher spewed enough venom with his penning of acerbic articles in the Atlanta newspaper, Bryant knew the value and power of that particular market to the Southeastern Conference.

When then Tech AD Doug Weaver approached the SEC about regaining entry into the league, he was told the league's ADs would have the initial say before it went any farther. The then 10-team league cast its ballots and Tech received four votes— one being from Alabama. For the moment, the issue of expansion for the SEC was dead, but Tech would find a new home in the ACC, and when the Southeastern Conference decided to expand its horizons it was too late for the olive branch to be extended to Tech.

On the eve of the 1979 game, Bryant took time to talk to Alf Van Hoose about the legendary Georgia Tech coach Bobby Dodd, the man responsible for much of Tech's national prominence and unfortunately the one who momentarily wrecked Tech's football appeal by pulling out of the nation's preeminent football league. "I always said we had to outwork Bobby Dodd because I couldn't outcoach him on Saturday," Bryant was telling a collection of reporters on the eve of the game. "I've always said Bobby was the best game day coach there ever was.

"I've remained friends with Bobby through the years. I played golf at the Atlanta Classic, attended a Braves game and spoke at the Atlanta TD Club. I saw Bobby at one of those events and we talked about renewing the series, feeling it was good for both schools. That's how it was scheduled."

For the record, Bryant was 7-2 in head-to-head matches with Dodd during those heated days of the series.

Pepper Spices Up the Day

After a series of coaches failed to reignite the fire in the Tech program, the Yellow Jackets turned to one of their own, Pepper Rodgers, who had generated enthusiasm into a moribund program at Kansas before taking UCLA to the upper echelon of the Pac-10.

Rodgers, on this day, was in his final year at Tech—he'd be axed at the end of the season in favor of Bill Curry, a future Alabama coach. One of Rodgers's assistants was an aspiring young coach named Steve Spurrier, who would in time dominate the SEC for a decade like Bryant did for a quarter-century.

Even the effervescent Rodgers, known for his antics on and off the field, was in awe of the legendary coach from Alabama. "I started to go over there and sing 'Yea, Alabama' to him," sighed Rodgers—who indeed can belt out the fight song word for word. "Really, I wanted to ask for his autograph, but I didn't have enough courage to ask him."

Practice viewers, who had proclaimed this might be the best Bryant team ever, were on target for the season opener. ABC again was there to televise the Tide, using one of its two opportunities with the season opener, and the Bama defense wrecked Tech's offense totally in the first half, limiting the Jackets to one first down and 41yards for the entire two quarters.

"I mean come on; that's unbelievable," said Rodgers. "I didn't think anyone could shut us down like that. They intimidated us, completely intimidated us."

Starting from its own four on a first-quarter drive, the Yellow Jackets managed four yards to move to eight, setting up the only first-half highlight for the home team.

Quarterback Mike Kelley quick-kicked, hitting an 80-yard punt that pushed the Alabama offense all the way back to its 12-yard line, but Kelley's rising star dove from the sky a few minutes later when E. J. Junior picked off one of his passes and raced 59 yards for the first touchdown of the season.

"It was teamwork," said Junior of his score. "Byron Braggs, Wayne Hamilton, and Randy Scott all made great blocks and made it pretty easy for me."

After an eight-minute drive that reached the Tech 14 resulted in zilch for points when Alan McElroy's field goal missed to the right, it appeared Tech would survive the half trailing by a mere 6-0, but Bama would get one more chance and backup quarterback Don Jacobs would engineer a 66-yard drive in 11 plays.

Major Ogilvie scored the first offensive TD of the year, but the try for two was no good and Bama led 12-0 at the half.

Leaving the field, ABC's sideline reporter Bill Flemming grabbed the coach and asked, "Coach Bryant, why did you take Shealy out?"

"To let the other boy [Don Jacobs] play," retorted Bryant.

As Flemming was asking question, he turned his mike to an open spot. Bryant was headed to the locker room. "Coach Bryant was always one of my favorite coaches," Flemming would later say. "I always enjoyed coming to Tuscaloosa to do my annual SEC show, and he was always as congenial as he could be, but on game day, he wasn't much into those halftime interviews."

The Wishbone Show

In the third quarter, Alabama held the football nearly 12 minutes, scored 15 points, had a fourth-down stop with Tech needing a few inches for a first at the Bama nine, and displayed the overall superiority it would exhibit for the first five weeks of the season.

On the first drive of the quarter, Shealy wheeled his team 54 yards in seven plays with Steve Whitman powering the final 13 for a TD that made it 19-0.

When Braggs slammed down Ronnie Cone well short of a first on the Bama nine, Shealy flawlessly operated the wishbone for 91 yards in 11 plays, keeping it himself five times, including the final 11 for the score, and hitting three passes, two to his roommate Keith Pugh and the other to Ogilvie. "For an old gimpy-legged quarterback, they weren't bad runs," said Shealy in his postgame interview.

Billy Jackson's run for two upped the lead to 27-0 and that was that, except for a fourth quarter field goal by McElroy and Tech's improbable score.

Alabama's shutout seemed assured when Robbie Jones intercepted Kelley with :32 left in the game, but the Tide linebacker

Steadman Shealy engineering the wishbone vs. Tech.
(Photo courtesy of the University of Alabama Archives)

fumbled it back to Tech at the Tide 39. With 12 ticks left on the clock, Kelley lofted a pass to Leon Chadwick in the end zone and as Braggs said, the Tech band struck up "The Ramblin' Wreck" fight song.

The Interception Party Begins

"We set a goal of setting the school record for interceptions," said secondary coach Bill "Brother" Oliver. "We gave up too many big plays in the passing game in 1978 and we had a group that was eager to rectify that problem."

Against the Spurrier pass brigade, Alabama intercepted four, with Junior and Jones being joined by Don McNeal and Gary DeNiro in picking off Kelley.

One player who didn't get a steal on the day but who made six tackles was freshman safety Tommy Wilcox, a converted quarterback. "I'd played quarterback throughout the spring. I like playing in the secondary. It's fun chasing and hitting people, instead of having them chase and hit me. I only want to help the team. If Coach Bryant wants me at quarterback, I'll play quarterback. If he wants me on defense, I'll play defense."

Even Bisher Impressed

In describing the Alabama defense in his Sunday column, long-time Bryant antagonist Bisher came away in awe of this defense: "You should be reminded Tech was playing a defense that plays like it is a mortal sin to give up a point." He would not be the last one impressed, either.

In the Alabama interview area, Bryant seemed to miss the days when the game was a marquee matchup in college football. "Naw, this wasn't as intense as it used to be," said Bryant. "I wish Tech was back in the Southeastern Conference. The game would mean a lot more then to both teams."

What kind of day was it for Rodgers? "I guess it is that type of day," said Rodgers when he meandered through 35 reporters and couldn't locate his missing seat. He just plopped down on his behind on the hard, hot concrete in the corner of the room and held court with the press.

Stephenson Honored

Alabama's center, Dwight Stephenson, was something special. Just ask Steadman Shealy, who said, "It was just an honor playing with him. He came in as a defensive end and he couldn't outbench press me. He became the greatest center in the history of the game. Coach Bryant had the unique ability to know where a player should be playing. Before the '77 season, he moved Terry Jones, an all-conference center to nose tackle and turned it over to Dwight. He wrote his own history."

Jack Rutledge, one of the line coaches who also helped coach John Hannah, agreed, "We had a lot of great centers, but Dwight was something special."

After the Georgia Tech game, Stephenson was feted by the AP as the Southeast's Lineman of the Week.

Chapter 18

The Bear Trap for the Bears

*"In all my years of coaching, this is the best defensive
team I've coached against, and I've coached against some
good ones at Texas, Penn State and many others."*
—Baylor Coach Grant Teaff after the 45-0 loss to Alabama

Paul Bryant, who had long ago earned the sobriquet of Bear
when he wrestled one back in Fordyce, Ark., as a strapping teenager, was storming around like a caged one the week of the Tide's
home opener against the Baylor Bears.

"Coach Bryant said it was the worst week of practice he'd
ever seen," said defensive tackle Byron Braggs. "He kept warning
us about Baylor and they were set to put a trap on us."

Indeed, the Bears, 2-0 on the year, landed in Legion Field
filled with optimism of upsetting the second-ranked Crimson
Tide. The week before Baylor had beaten Texas A&M and the
Bears had closed the '78 season with a stunning 38-14 win over
Texas.

"From watching Baylor on film, I knew it was going to be a
tough game," said running back Major Ogilvie. "I really thought
if we scored 17 points on their defense it would be a good night."

If there was any complacency with the players or the over-flow crowd of 77,512, it quickly abated when Simpson Pepper, the longtime PA announcer, said a final score: Texas A&M 27, Penn State 14.

"I'd been impressed with Baylor on film, too," said Braggs. "When I heard that score from State College, I knew we'd better buckle up the chin straps. I was ready."

Turnovers to Points

In the first half, Alabama didn't exactly scintillate, turning it over three times, allowing Baylor to stay somewhat in the game, though with the battering the Bears' offense was taking, the 14 points the Tide did score probably would have lasted for 10 more games.

E. J. Junior's blocked punt in the first quarter was recovered by David Hannah at Baylor's 28, but the Tide had to settle for a 30-yard field goal by Alan McElroy.

Later in the quarter, Don McNeal started the interception parade by picking off Mickey Elam at midfield. Steadman Shealy steered the Tide to the seven where the drive stalled and McElroy kicked another field goal to make it 6-0.

On its next possession, the Tide scored a TD, with Shealy breaking free and racing 54 yards to the Baylor 10, setting up a score on the next play, a run by Billy Jackson. Shealy passed to Ogilive for the two to make it 14-0.

A Second-Half Blitz

In the third quarter, Baylor ran a total of six plays to Alabama's 26, and that pretty much tells you what happened. One of those eight-minute drives by Bama erased better than half the quarter. It was a 16-play, 70-yarder that ended with McElroy's third field goal of the game, upping the lead to 17-0.

Taking over with a tick under 4:00 left in the third, the Tide backups ran out the third-quarter clock, ending the quarter with the ball on the Baylor five-yard line. A 16-yard run by Mark Nix and a 14-yard keeper by Jacobs had moved Bama deep into Bear territory, and on the first play of the fourth quarter Nix opened the floodgates of a 28-point period when he scored from the two.

Nix scored again, this time from the four, to make it 31-0, ending a six-play, 61-yard drive. After a Bobby Smith interception and with the third quarterback Alan Gray in the game, Joe Jones got in the scoring act, bulling over left guard to make it 38-0.

John Hill finished the scoring with a 10-yard run to make it 45-0. Alabama had run a record 82 times for the day for 453 yards. Alabama had amassed 24 first downs to Baylor's six, and only one of those came in the second half.

"The game was won where it's supposed to be won, on the line of scrimmage," said Bryant who then contradicted himself by adding, "We really never did establish anything. We never found anything that we could go back to."

Alabama center Dwight Stephenson gave the credit for the unimaginably easy victory to Bryant: "All of Coach Bryant's game plans are good, but this one was special."

Baylor's Teaff was still in awe about what had transpired at Legion Field, telling the press, "Alabama is the best defensive team I've ever faced. Alabama is the most balanced football team I've ever seen. Period. I'm not talking about offensive balance. I'm talking about offense-defense and the kicking game."

On the official stat rushing charts, there is room for ten players and the Bama stat crew had to add a line of its own because 11 different backs carried it, with Shealy leading the way with 86 yards on 13 carries and Ogilvie getting 73 on 15. Eight of the backs had at least one rush for 10 or more yards. It had been some kind of performance.

Don McNeal played the perfect game vs. Baylor.
(Photo courtesy of The University of Alabama Archives)

SEC Players of the Week

The Tide's supremacy over Baylor didn't go unnoticed by Ed Shearer, the Southeast's AP sports editor, as he picked E. J. Junior and Jim Bunch as the co-SEC Linemen of the Week and Don McNeal as the Back of the Week.

Bunch had the unenviable assigned task for much of the game of taking on Baylor All-American and future Hall of Famer Mike Singletary, and although the Bear linebacker had 13 tackles, all of them were after gains of five or more yards.

But Bunch didn't think that much of his play, telling Shearer, "Why did they give it to me? I think every linemen we had deserved it. Coach Bryant says Steve Whitman is the most underrated player in the SEC. I think it is Vince Boothe. Dwight Stephenson, Mike Brock, Vince and Buddy Aydelette all deserved to be the linemen of the week. We dominated a good Baylor defense."

After returning an interception for a TD against Georgia Tech, Junior blocked a punt and had two sacks against the Golden Bear offense. Then there was McNeal being one of six Crimson Tide players to intercept, his being the first in the first quarter.

McNeal deflected the praise like he did passes, saying: "To play what the coaches call a perfect game is gratifying. We had six interceptions and I only had one. The entire defense dominated."

How well did McNeal play that September 22 night? He scored a rare 100 percent, earning this praise from his head coach Paul Bryant, who told Shearer, "We've had a few on defense to do it, but it's very unusual. Lee Roy [Jordan] did it a time or two, maybe three, but we have had many others. He had 14 bonus points. He took out the blocking back on E. J. Junior's blocked punt. It's the little things that make the big plays."

Six More Picks

After the Tide started the season with four interceptions against Georgia Tech, it upped the total by two against the Bears with Tommy Wilcox, Ricky Tucker, Bobby Smith, and Wayne Hamilton joining McNeal in the pickoff department.

Fumble recoveries by defensive backs Mike Clements and Ken Coley added to the rout that early autumn evening. If Junior's blocked punt had counted in the turnover department, which it didn't, Bama would have had nine for the night. Eight was good enough.

"That defensive team was something special," said linebacker coach Jeff Rouzie. "They had the unique capacity to make big play after big play. We also had a few sacks on the quarterback as well. It was a near-perfect performance."

Actually, the Tide had six sacks, with Byron Braggs leading the assault with three for a minus 17, Junior getting his two, and Gary DeNiro adding the final one.

Teaff tried three different quarterbacks, and the Tide defense treated them equally, picking off Elam, Mike Brannan, and Steve Smith twice apiece. For the night Baylor dropped back to pass 28, completing five, having six intercepted and being sacked the six times.

Chapter 19

Sinking the Commodores

"I've seen a lot of great teams, but I don't think I've ever seen a more complete team than Alabama. I thought they were the best team coming into this game, and I can tell you after what I've witnessed, they may be the best team I've ever seen."
—Vanderbilt coach George MacIntyre

Only those with a myopic view of college football could have accused Paul Bryant of running up the score against Vanderbilt September 29, 1979, though the 66-3 score certainly seemed to indicate such a trouncing.

"Coach Bryant had an affection for Vanderbilt dating back to his days as an assistant coach there," said Kirk McNair, the one-time Bryant SID and longtime editor of *Bama Magazine*. "He didn't like embarrassing anyone, especially Vandy."

If the stat crew at Legion Field was scrambling for room to insert all the players the week before against Baylor, the Vanderbilt number folks really had overtime duty.

Fourteen different Alabama running backs carried the ball.

Thirty different Alabama defensive players were credited with at least one tackle.

Nine different Alabama players scored.

"About the only disappointing thing was Vandy scoring," said Byron Braggs. "We flat don't like people scoring on us. As far as I'm concerned, we didn't do our job. We let 'em get a field goal in the first half. That isn't good."

Indeed, the Commodores had booted a field goal in the first half, but it was 32-3 at the halfway point. Alabama scored early and often with Steadman Shealy speeding untouched 65 yards on the Tide's second offensive play.

Then it was Major Ogilvie cruising in from the eight, but he took a major lick that stunned him. "I'm on the bench, trying to get my senses," said Ogilvie. "Jerry Duncan [the sideline radio man] came over and asked me how I was doing. I told him, 'I'll live, Jerry.'

"Jerry repeated it to John Forney and Doug Layton on the radio broadcast. On Monday, I had a note to see Coach Bryant. I didn't have a clue what it was about. He told me he didn't want me smarting off on the bench. I didn't even know what he was talking about until someone told me what I'd said. I certainly wasn't trying to be smart, but Coach didn't see it quite that way."

Vanderbilt averted the shutout with a late first-quarter, early second-quarter drive. In reality, it was a 31-yard burst by quarterback Van Heflin on an option play that set up a 47-yard field goal by Mike Woodard.

The rout was then officially on. In short order, Alabama scored in the following manner:

Shealy scored on a keeper from the 19 and then hit Ogilvie on a two-point pass to make it 22-3.

Then the Tide's second team went the length of the field but had to settle for a short 21-yard field goal by Alan McElroy.

Now it was the third team's chance after Wayne Hamilton forced a fumble at the Vandy 21. With Alan Gray at quarterback, Mark Nix did scoring honors from the one, making it 32-3 at the half.

*Don McNeal(28) and Jim Bob Harris (9) were like most of the
starters, wearing visors and watching from the sidelines in Nashville.
(Photo courtesy of the University of Alabama Archives)*

Even the Backup Kickers Score

The first team got its only action of the second half on the first series, and Shealy guided the team 56 yards in seven plays, with Steve Whitman barrelling into the end zone from the three. McElroy's PAT was no good, leaving it at 38-3.

Don Jacobs took over for Shealy and broke free on a 51-yard run to spark an 85-yard march that culminated with Joe Jones scoring from the one to up it to 45-3.

With Gray back at the helm, Alabama started at its 20 before moving to Vandy's 29 as the third quarter ended. Jones scored his second TD, taking a pitch from Gray at the three for the next TD. Joining the scoring parade was wide receiver and kickoff man Tim Clark, who kicked the extra point to make it 52-3.

A Landmark Series

With 9:44 left in the fourth quarter, offensive coordinator Mal Moore inserted Michael Landrum into the game at quarterback. A freshman from Sweet Water, Ala., Landrum, wearing No. 12—the same jersey worn by such previous luminaries as Pat Trammell, Joe Namath, Kenny Stabler, and Scott Hunter—became the first black quarterback for the Tide.

"I started getting butterflies after the managers gave me a tearaway jersey," said Landrum after the game. "When I first went out there, I was a little shaky. But after a couple of plays, I felt better."

Landrum failed to move the team the first time he was in the game, but the next time he guided the team 25 yards for a score. He completed a pass to the third-team quarterback and fourth-team receiver Gray for 13 yards to move the chains on third down, setting up a three-yard run by Landrum for the touchdown.

Continuing to use everyone available, Bryant now subbed Joe Jones as the extra point kicker, and he converted to make it 59-3.

Mercifully, Vandy's despairing day ended when John Hill took a Landrum handoff and scored from 14 yards out. And again, Jones kicked the PAT, making it 66-3.

Visor Day in Nashville

Alabama's starters played so seldom that most donned visors while staring into the sun. "About the only pictures they got of the starters were us on the bench with those visors," said Braggs. "It was a day for the subs to get their chance. Like I said, I wasn't too happy because we let them score."

Center Dwight Stephenson was more spectator than participant as well.

"To tell the truth, the score got out of hand early and we were playing fourth stringers. I wanted everyone to play well and I think they did, but it got out of hand."

QBs & Interceptions

Alabama's four quarterbacks—Shealy, Jacobs, Gray and Landrum—carried collectively 14 times for 160 yards. Shealy had 75 on four carries and Jacobs 71 also on four tries.

Hill was the leading gainer for the day, netting 87 on 10 carries.

For the game, Alabama netted 601 yards, including 471 on the ground.

Bobby Smith's interception in the second quarter upped the Tide's total to 11, two shy of the entire total of the '78 national champs. Backup defensive ends Mike Pitts and John Mauro had five tackles apiece.

"Alabama's wishbone run is difficult enough to stop, but Alabama's ability to pass out of it, getting the one-on-one situations, makes it almost impossible to stop them," said MacIntyre.

"About the only thing that can slow them down is some injuries, and I don't know if that will stop them based on what I saw today."

Tight end Bart Krout earned his first start due to an injury to Tim Travis, an ominous sign of the weeks to come when the injuries would mount and almost derail the championship express.

Chapter 20

No Shock Here

*"Most players are lucky if they go through one goal-
line stand in a lifetime, I've been through several.
We just don't like people scoring on us."*
—Defensive lineman Curtis McGriff after the Wichita State game

When SMU—then a legit power in the now defunct Southwest Conference—reneged on its deal to come to Alabama to
play the Crimson Tide, Coach Paul Bryant instructed his chief
administrator Sam Bailey to put out an all points bulletin to find
an opponent for the Tide on October 6.

There was only one taker, the Wichita State Shockers, a team
seeking a $100,000 paycheck and knowing the impossible odds
of winning at Tuscaloosa. Coach Jeff Jeffries's Shockers had one
goal it wanted to achieve: to score a touchdown against the vaunted
Alabama defense.

And the Shockers would get that chance late in the third
quarter. Starting from its own nine, WSU quarterback Prince
McJunkins regally marched his Shockers down the field. Of course,
the score was 35-0 at that point, and a roughing on a third and
15 had sustained the drive.

On third and three from the Bama 42, McJunkins kept it on the option, and wheeled upfield with nothing but green and a TD in sight. If McJunkins was determined to score, Alabama safety Jim Bob Harris was equally resolute in his will to keep him out of the end zone. Harris's grit paid off, stopping McJunkins just inside the one-yard line.

"We are taught to never give up on a play, that each play may make the difference," Harris told reporters after the game. "After I caught him, the big guys took over on the goal line."

In the middle of the goal-line defense was noseman Warren Lyles, who was flanked by Byron Braggs and Curtis McGriff, who noted, "I looked at Warren Lyles before the first play and I told him to drive the center back, so Byron and I would have room to operate. We did and the quarterback had no room to run. After that all the pressure was on them, not us."

Braggs bagged McJunkins on the first-down sneak, actually knocking him back a foot.

Again McJunkins sneaked on second down, only to be forced back by linebacker Randy Scott and McGriff. "It was getting fun," said McGriff. "I didn't think they'd run another sneak on third, but he did."

And the results were the same, as Scott and Wayne Hamilton collaborated this time to shove him back yet another foot.

Now, facing fourth down from just outside the one, the Prince opted to head toward the left, only be greeted rather harshly by E. J. Junior, who not only smashed McJunkins backwards but knocked the ball loose in the process. Ricky Tucker recovered the fumble on the four, and that was that.

"Those four plays brought back a lot of memories of the Sugar Bowl," said McGriff.

"We want shutouts," said Braggs. "It's part of our tradition, and we just don't like it when someone else scores."

"The crowd really picked it up and it was like the Sugar Bowl all over again," responded Hamilton. "Them scoring never entered our minds."

"We ran the same defense, more or less, on all four plays," said David Hannah. "A goal-line stand is the biggest thrill a defensive player can have. It means a lot to the pride of the team when a team is a foot from the goal and can't score."

Jeffries Thanked the Bear

After the game Jeffries thanked Bryant for being charitable in not running up the score against his outmanned team. "Coach Bryant played it conservatively in the second half and ran everybody he had on the bench into the game," said Jeffries. "I don't know if they tried a pass in the second half; if they did, I don't recall it."

Alabama scored early and often in the first half, rolling to a 28-0 lead with Steadman Shealy doing the damage in the first quarter on a 27-yard pass to Keith Pugh and scoring himself from three yards out. Major Ogilvie scored twice in the second quarter, including a four-yard rush that ended an 87-yard, 11-play drive.

On its opening drive of the third quarter, Shealy again methodically marched the Tide down the field, covering 75 yards in 10 plays, and the Tide quarterback scored from the eight to finish the TD parade on this day. Backup running back and backup kicker Joe Jones hit the final extra point to make it 35-0, and Alan McElroy's field goal upped the final margin to 38-0.

Interesting View from an Auburn Player

While Alabama was dismantling Wichita State, cross-state rival Auburn was beating a talented North Carolina State that featured All-American center Jim Richter, the leading candidate for the Outland Trophy, signifying the best lineman in the nation.

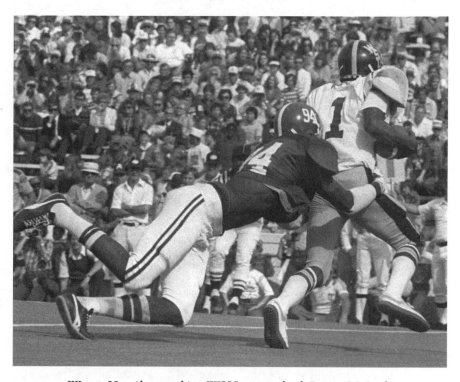

Wayne Hamilton sacking WSU quarterback Prince McJunkins.
(Photo courtesy of the University of Alabama Archives)

Auburn's Marvin Williams had a different take on the situation. "Did he win the Outland last year?" Williams asked. "I'll give him credit, he's a good player, but he's not in the same league as Dwight Stephenson. He's not close to being the best center in the nation. Stephenson is."

Death in the Family

Before the game, the father of tight end Tim Travis passed away in Bessemer. "The Lord gave me strength to play," a distressed Travis said.

"If I hadn't played I would have let my dad down."

After his traditional spiel about being out-coached, Bryant lowered his voice and talked about Travis's loss. "I want to point this out," said Bryant. "It's been a very difficult few days for Tim Travis. He lost his dad and the funeral is tomorrow. I really didn't expect him to play, but he wanted to play for his father and to be with his teammates. He told me that's what his dad would have wanted, for him to be with his Alabama family."

Alabama Continues to be Second in the Polls

In its first four games, the Alabama defense had allowed a last-second TD pass to Georgia Tech and a field goal to Vanderbilt, but the Tide was still second and not gaining on Southern California in the polls.

It irked middle guard Lyles to no end, and he vented his opinion to the press. "Let's face it, there's a lot of prejudice against Alabama and a lot of people dislike Coach Bryant and a lot of people dislike Alabama just because they know we don't back down to anyone. We don't take anybody lightly and no one takes us lightly, and we like it that way."

Chapter 21

The Swamp Awash with a Crimson Tide

*"Today, Alabama was far superior to any team I've
ever seen. Ever. I don't think it was possible for
anyone to dominate a game like they did."*
—Florida coach Charley Pell

If there was a peak moment in the 1979 season and it wasn't
the rout of Baylor, then it had to be the flood of the swamp in
Gainesville. If there is such a score of 40-0 not indicating how
badly a team was thrashed, it had to be the Florida game.

Statistics can sometimes tell a misleading story . . . but not in
this case. From Alan McElroy's opening kickoff until John Hill
pounded 23 yards to the Gator 19 on the final play, this was a
story of Alabama football at its apex.

For the game, Alabama had 22 first downs to Florida's three.

The Tide ran off 78 plays to the Gators' 41.

The Crimsons totaled 454 yards to the orange and blue's 66.

Bama converted 10 of 15 third downs and two of two on
fourth; UF moved the chains once in 11 third down tries.

Florida's only completion, a seven-yarder to future NFL star Cris Collinsworth in the first quarter, resulted in the Gator star being unceremoniously slammed to the artificial surface by linebacker Randy Scott.

Yet despite the carnage on the field, it was the Alabama team that suffered a series of injuries that would create several weeks of offensive angst for the Tide. "Keith Pugh separated a shoulder," said quarterback Steadman Shealy. "We had a number of other injuries, but that one really affected our offense. He was the key to our passing attack, and with him out, we faced a series of teams that took advantage of it."

Alabama's wishbone didn't need its wings on this day, as the offensive line and running backs pushed the Gators all over Florida Field.

The Fake Punt

Shealy scored on the first series of the game after his backup Don Jacobs converted a fourth and eight from the Florida 34 with a 25-yard ramble to the nine on a fake punt.

"It's the only idea I've had in 10 years," Paul Bryant told the press about the fake punt in the third quarter. "It was mine. We put it in for Penn State for the Sugar Bowl and didn't get to use it because we got a delay penalty. It was Sylvester Croom's idea to put it in for Florida. They ran nine players in there and they didn't have a clue of what we'd done. I could have kissed him on that play."

"I got to the line and saw we had them outnumbered on their left side and I just took off," said Jacobs. "I really didn't have to do much."

Later in the quarter, Shealy commanded an 85-yard drive, finishing it off with a handoff to fullback Steve Whitman at the five. A 31-yard field goal by McElroy with :31 left in the half made it 17-0.

Another Jacobs Moment

Leading 17-0, Bryant subbed his second team early in the third quarter, and Jacobs made the most of his opportunity, taking the snap and breaking free for a 73-yard TD run—which would be the longest of the season for the Crimson Tide.

A few minutes later the first team was back in for a more conventional wishbone drive, six straight runs with Major Ogilvie scoring from the one and McElroy, who had missed the PAT after Jacobs's score, making it 30-0.

The third unit got its chance with 1:56 left in the third and after 14 rushes, including seven by quarterback Alan Gray, the Tide scored on a Hill run of two with 10:11 left in the game.

McElroy finished the scoring with a 34-yard field goal after fourth-string quarterback Michael Landrum and his backup troops moved down to the Gator four, only be to penalized back to the 19.

Starting safety Tommy Wilcox picked off a Tyrone Young pass in the third quarter and backup sophomore cornerback Benny Perrin picked off quarterback Jonell Brown's pass on Florida's final offensive play, pushing the Tide season total to 14.

Worried and With Reason

Paul Bryant didn't need to wait for Goostree's injury update to realize the rout of Florida had come with a dear price. "I don't need a report," Bryant snarled. "All you have to do is look around and see all these players on crutches."

"I don't know if we ever had a team that started out like the '79 team," said Goostree. "We really hadn't been challenged at all, and here we are getting ready for a dangerous Tennessee team and we are all banged up. Coach Bryant would have been concerned no matter what. He's a born worrier, but he was more worried than normal."

Don Jacobs's fake punt set the Tide on a roll in the swamp.
(Photo courtesy of the University of Alabama Archives)

Back to No. 1

After getting word of Stanford's improbable tie with Southern California, Alabama's ascendancy to the top spot in the rankings seemed imminent, but Bryant—who cast a ballot on the UPI coaches' poll—couldn't shake his ever-increasing concern about his team and Tennessee.

Bryant talked more about Tennessee than the swamped Gators, telling those gathered around him at Florida Field, "Bill Oliver will be in charge of the game plan for Tennessee and I'm sure he'll do a good job. Tennessee is awfully hungry to beat us, probably more so than anyone else, and that is saying a mouthful, 'cause there's a lot of folks eager to whip us."

"This is the most crippled team I've ever had, that's why I'm not voting us No. 1," Bryant said upon returning from Gainesville. "Right now I've got Nebraska, Texas, Alabama, Ohio State, Houston, Florida State, Arkansas, Brigham Young and Southern Cal.

"I'm not concerned where we are right now. I'd ten times rather have our team healthy than be No. 1. It's hard enjoying being No. 1 under the circumstances. Go look at all our players on crutches and ask me how I feel."

When the polls did come out, Alabama was No. 1 for the first time followed by Texas, Nebraska, Southern Cal, Houston, Ohio State, Florida State, Oklahoma, Notre Dame and Arkansas.

The Sack Pack & Crossing the 50

How efficient was the Tide defense this October 13? Besides two interceptions and a fumble recovery, Alabama sacked the Gators five times, threw running backs for losses three more times, and allowed only one play of more than eight yards, that coming on a quarterback scramble by Young in the second quarter for Florida's only conversion of the day. Remember, too, the Gators only ran 41 plays from the line of scrimmage.

Florida crossed the midfield stripe once on this overcast, windy day where the temperatures reached a high of 75 degrees, and that penetration into Tide territory didn't last long.

An interception turned the ball over to Florida at its own 49. On the opening play of the third, the Gators penetrated Tide territory when Gordon Pleasants plowed ahead for two to the Bama 49 on first down, where Tommy Wilcox stopped him. A host of white shirts stopped Terry Williams at the 48 on second down.

Facing a third and seven, quarterback Tyrone Young dropped back to pass, only to be sacked by David Hannah for a nine-yard loss back at the Gator 43. No Florida drive ended on Bama's side of the field the entire afternoon.

Besides Hannah, linebacker Randy Scott, end E. J. Junior, end Mike Pitts, and tackle Curtis McGriff had sacks. Junior also had a tackle behind the line, as did Thomas Boyd and Wayne Hamilton. Wilcox and Perrin had picks and reserve defensive back Ken Coley had a fumble recovery. Offensively, 13 different backs carried the ball, with Jacobs netting 122 on seven carries.

Duncan Dilemma

Alabama's radio crew of John Forney, Doug Layton and Jerry Duncan incurred a most embarrassing situation, especially for Duncan, when the trio tried to jet from Birmingham to Gainesville the Friday before the game.

"I'd been hunting a few weeks ago and I left a .22 pistol in my bag," said Duncan.

"When I was going through a checkpoint, those machines just starting beeping and before I knew it the police, the security and even the FBI were there.

"I watched John and Doug go to the plane, and I kept telling them I had to get to the football game. Well, the first plane took off without me and I was detained and being interrogated.

"I finally got on a plane and got down there. To say I was the butt of a lot of jokes would be an understatement." The key to his "release" was telling him Coach Bryant wanted him in Gainesville. Those words spoke volumes and extricated Duncan from the scrutiny of the enforcement agents.

Chapter 22

This is Alabama Football, the Comeback

".... It's a crystal blue autumn afternoon in Birmingham, Alabama, and a fine day for football on the third Saturday in October. And today on a sun-drenched Legion Field, Paul Bryant's No. 1-rated Alabama Crimson Tide will host its time-honored foe, the Tennessee Volunteers, coached by Johnny Majors in this renewal of this classic rivalry."
—John Forney, the Voice of the Tide, on October 20, 1979

Even John Forney, long an ally to Paul Bryant, didn't realize his introduction would prophesy a classic Bryant production—his team reeling from an early Tennessee assault but finding within their inner beings the resolve to rally for a victory the coach would personally rank among his own list of favorites.

The first quarter was a virtual lurid orange flash as the sky-high Volunteers rocked the top off the aging edifice on Graymont Avenue in Birmingham. A Steadman Shealy fumble on the first series signaled an ominous warning of what was to come, though the nation's premier defense quickly forced the Vols to punt back, but the Big Orange had wrested away field position, pushing Bama back to its own 12.

"I can truthfully say it was the worst game I ever played," said Shealy, who missed an exchange with fullback Steve Whitman on the Volunteer 14, and suddenly Tennessee was deep in Tide territory.

Two runs netted three yards, but on third down quarterback Jimmy Streater hit Phil Ingram at the back of the end zone with 7:54 left in the quarter and Alan Duncan's PAT not only gave UT a 7-0 lead but placed the Tide behind for the first time for the season.

After the offense failed to move again, Streater engineered the first real scoring drive of the year against the previously impenetrable Bama "D."

Starting from their own 37, the Volunteers converted a key third down on a run by Streater and sustained it again on a pass to running back Hubert Simpson for 15 yards that moved it to Bama's 14. There would be no goal-line stand here, as three straight runs had the Vols in the end zone, with Streater appropriately doing the honors from the three, the first rushing TD of the year against the Tide. Duncan's extra point gave Tennessee 14 points, one more than the first five opponents had scored.

Momentum continued to be clad in orange and white, as Shealy was sacked on a third-down pass attempt to force a Woody Umphrey punt on the final play of the first quarter, and the Vols opened the second quarter at their own 47.

The Defense Begins to Exert Itself

Streater continued to inflict daggers into the heart of the Bama defense, as he ran and passed the Vols to the Tide 24, where finally the "Redwood Forest" exerted the pressure . . . and it would shadow the Orange the rest of the day.

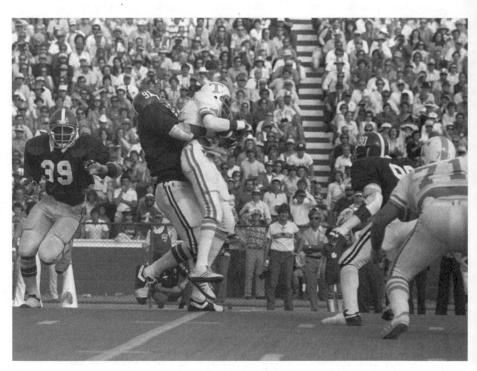

Warren Lyles sacks UT's Silver Streak.
(Photo courtesy of the University of Alabama Archives)

Warren Lyles smothered Streater, known as the"Silver Streak," for a sack to shove the Vols back to the 28, but Duncan's 45-yard field goal was good, making it 17-0 and dimming the hopes of the majority of the 77,665 fans crammed into Legion Field.

With Shealy struggling, Bryant turned to Don Jacobs, and the backup quarterback started the first real offensive movement of the day, pitching to Major Ogilvie for a 26-yard gain on first down. But the Tide's hopes were doused again when Jacobs fumbled at the UT 27, the third turnover of the first half by a team that entered the game leading the nation in turnover margin.

"It was time to show them some Alabama football," said tackle Byron Braggs, and his sidekicks David Hannah and Warren Lyles chased Streater, forcing a pass that Lyles tipped and Robbie Jones intercepted at the UT 33.

"It was time for the offense to do something, and we went to the air," said Shealy.

"Tim Travis had a great game in Knoxville in '78, scoring twice on end run options," said offensive coordinator Mal Moore. "We'd moved the ball on the last drive and felt we'd hit 'em with the tight end pass."

Travis was wide open across the middle and Shealy hit him in stride for a 33-yard TD. McElroy's extra point made it 17-7.

Neither team effectively moved the rest of the half, with Tommy Wilcox sacking Streater for a 12-yard loss and forcing him to fumble out of bounds on the final play of the half.

The Halftime Pep Talk

"When Coach Bryant came into the locker room, I was scared to death what he was going to say," said Braggs. "He was smiling. I couldn't believe it. He said we've got them right where we want them. I thought he'd lost it. He then talked about character and if we had it, we'd respond like champions. We were all pumped by his speech. Tennessee didn't know what was getting ready to hit them."

"In those days the locker room at Legion Field was pretty cramped," said Ogilvie. "We were broken down in our offensive area, and Coach [Moore] and Coach [Dee] Powell were frantically diagramming what Tennessee was doing on the board. We could sense Coach Bryant's presence before we ever saw him.

"He just came over and said give me that chalk, and then he erased everything they had written on the board. Coach Moore and Coach Powell just kind of moved out of the way. Coach Bryant said, 'Just go out there, hang on to the football and knock them off the ball and we'll be all right.' Coach Moore and Coach Powell just said, 'You heard what he said.'

"We went out there and took it to them."

In the postgame interviews, David Hannah, the last of the fabled Hannah family to play for the Tide, told the press: "In the first half, Tennessee made us realize we're not nearly as good as we thought we were. They did to us exactly what we needed to do to them, control the game from the opening kickoff.

"Our dressing room was quiet, almost somber. Coach Bryant reacted in a way that shows why he is so great. He didn't blow his cool. He merely explained the situation and told us what was expected of us. Then, right before we went back on the field, E. J. Junior, Warren Lyles and I got together and prayed. The Lord was good enough to help us win."

The Second Half was Bama's

Inspired by Bryant's halftime histrionics, Alabama drowned any hopes of a Tennessee upset. Ricky Tucker's interception enabled the offense to start from the Volunteer 30, and Ogilvie concluded the six-play drive with a one-yard run.

On its next possession, Jacobs engineered a 14-play, 70-yard drive that ended with Ogilvie's second TD, this one on a six-yard run on a third-down play. "Major knows only one way to run, and that is north and south, and this time he was headed south," barked out Doug Layton after Forney had screamed over the noise of the crowd that the Major had scored.

In the fourth quarter, it was Jacobs taking the Tide 80 yards, again on 14 plays, 13 of them runs with Jacobs scoring the clincher from the 13-yard line.

"We had a wishbone right play in the huddle," said Jacobs after the game. "I saw Tennessee defense cheat to the right, so I decided I'd take it myself. I just took the snap and ran. I gambled and won. Our offensive line had a lot to do with it. Shoot, we had driven from our 20 to get that far. The line was doing a great job."

Taking over a few minutes later, Jacobs and the Tide again methodically started a roll down the field, and with each run seconds ticked away until there were no more and Alabama was sitting within the shadows of the Volunteer end zone.

A Championship Team

"I think Alabama is a championship team now," said Bryant. "I didn't know before the game, but I know now. We went into this game with a lot of injuries. I think when we get some of those folks back we can beat anybody in the country. This was one of the greatest comebacks I've ever been associated with. It was one of the greatest comebacks anyone will ever have against Tennessee."

Ogilvie, who gained 109 yards on 13 carries, summed it up this way: "I bet we gave the crowd a scare. But you know what, we gave ourselves a pretty good scare, too. I'll tell you, though, we never gave up. We felt we could win this game all along. It was just a matter of doing the things we do best. Coach Bryant is the greatest coach for a reason. He coaches with poise and confidence. Those two things paid off for us today."

Tucker, whose interception pushed the team total to 16, simply put it: "You laugh at terms like self-pride, but that's what it was. It was poise, character and confidence."

How the Tide Responded

In the second half, Tennessee accumulated a net of 71 yards, finishing this day with 220, and the "Silver Streak," who was so brilliant early finished hitting only seven of 23 to go with two interceptions and nine passes being knocked down, including four by safety Jim Bob Harris. Conversely, the Tide rushed for 313 yards and passed for 83 more on its way to being No. 1 for the second straight week.

The Passing of H7is Coach

As jubilant as Bryant was about the dramatic comeback, he was equally moved by the news that his position coach at Alabama, Red Drew, had passed away in a Tuscaloosa nursing home the morning of October 20.

"I'm terribly sorry to hear the news about Coach Drew," said Bryant. "Coach Drew was my personal coach when I was at Alabama trying to be a player. He was one of the greatest people I've ever known. He was a real class person, and I loved him like a daddy. He meant a lot to football and a lot more to Alabama."

The First Appearance on ESPN

ABC-TV owned the rights to live telecasts during the 1970s, and by the regulations of the NCAA a team could appear five times over a two-year window. Alabama, by far the most appealing TV team in the South, had earned three appearances in '78 with Legion Field airings against Nebraska, USC and LSU, leaving it open for two games in '79.

Obviously, ABC had picked the Georgia Tech game, and the network's president Jim Spence indicated he had bypassed the Tennessee game in order to air the LSU contest.

There was a budding sports network in Bristol, Conn., called ESPN that was in its infancy and it decided to re-broadcast some games, including Alabama-Tennessee. Jim Simpson, a UA grad, traveled to Tuscaloosa to announce the game. It would be the first Tide debut, albeit on a delayed basis, that Alabama would appear on what would become sports' super station.

Bama Maintains No. 1

After the win over the Volunteers, the Crimson Tide maintained a comfortable advantage in the AP poll, netting 32-first place votes, while Nebraska and Southern California held on to the 2-3 spots, trailed by Arkansas and Ohio State.

Chapter 23

Bob Hope Lifts the
Spirits at Homecoming

*"Joe Namath got in late and he came into the room and I
asked him if he'd memorized his script and he laughed,
pulling it out of his pocket. Coach Bryant said, 'Bob, you
didn't ask me if I'd memorized mine.' I didn't tell him I
didn't have enough guts to ask him if he'd learned his. My
gosh, it was like telling God what to do."*
—Entertainer Bob Hope

The highlight of the 1979 Homecoming centered around an
appearance by renowned entertainer Bob Hope, who was on campus to film a segment for his NBC special, *Homecoming U.S.A.*
which also featured Indiana State, Colgate, Florida, Southern Cal,
and Harvard

"They shot the skit in the old A-Club Room in Memorial
Coliseum on Friday before the game," said Clem Gryska, then
an administrator and now a staff member at the Bryant Museum.
"Coach Bryant played the role of a coach, Joe Namath the part of
a former player who brings an aging kicker to campus, and of
course, Bob Hope played that role."

*Bob Hope, Joe Namath and Paul Bryant doing their skit for the NBC special.
(Photo courtesy of The University of Alabama Archives)*

Flying in from New York, Namath was late due to a delay in Atlanta, so Bryant and Hope exchanged stories for an hour or so before the legendary quarterback appeared.

When Namath entered the room, Hope asked, "Have you read your script, Joe?" Namath laughed and pointed at his pocket where the white sheets of paper were encamped. Namath laughed louder when Hope inquired if he had memorized it.

Even Bryant was laughing when he asked Hope why he hadn't asked him earlier if he'd learned his lines, to which Hope replied, "I'm too scared of you to ask you."

During the shooting of the skit, Hope, playing the role of "Thunderfoot," knocked over a figurine of an Alabama football player, smashing it in several shards on the table in which it had called home. Bryant simply said, "That's about how injured our team is now."

After the session, said Gryska, Coach Bryant hurried Namath up to his office for a visit while all of the assistant coaches got to visit with Bob Hope. It was a special Homecoming.

A Systematic Victory

For the second straight year, the Crimson Tide hosted Virginia Tech, then known as the Gobblers, for Homecoming, and it was a no-frills, not-much-of-a-thriller day.

After a scoreless first quarter, Don Jacobs and the second team concluded an 83-yard drive on a 48-yard pass to backup receiver Keith Marks, whose father Bobby just happened to be an assistant on the team.

With :51 left in the half, Steadman Shealy scored from the 14, ending a 72-play, 13-play drive, and it was 14-0 at the half.

Playing without the injured Major Ogilvie or Keith Pugh, the offense methodically drove 80 yards for a third quarter, with Shealy hurdling over the left side from the six, to make it 21-0.

Then, VPI did something no team had done all year – or would do—it traveled the length of the field, a full 80 yards, on a touchdown march, with quarterback Steve Casey, who had been intercepted in the end zone by Tommy Wilcox in the first half, scoring from the two.

"Their receiver had me beat," said Wilcox. "I saw the quarterback underthrow it enough for me to get it. Our goal every week is to shut the other team down and hold them to zero points. We try to get the goose egg, but it's hard against a good offense like VPI."

In the fourth quarter, E. J. Junior knocked the ball loose on an option play and recovered it at the Tide six to set up a two-yard score by Jeff Fagan and Alan McElroy's 23-yard field goal finalized the scoring at 31-7.

Bryant's 200th Win at UA

The victory over Tech was the 200th career win for Paul Bryant at his alma mater, but his increasing concerns about the injury status of his team negated any celebration.

"We had 13 players that didn't play today [including Ogilvie, Pugh, guard Mike Brock, defensive end Gary DeNiro, and full-back-halfback Billy Jackson].

"I thought our halfbacks played well under the circumstances. Some of them we played today hadn't even played at all this year, and the others only a few snaps. If Steve Whitman hadn't played at fullback, I don't know what we would we have done.

"I didn't even know about the 200th win, until some of the players mentioned it. A lot of people have contributed to all those wins—players, coaches, the press, the alumni, and a lot of mommas and poppas."

Disappointing Win?

Nose guard Warren Lyles expressed his displeasure with the effort of the defense and the seven points yielded. "We try to get

goose eggs in every game. I was disappointed that they scored on
the goal line. We're trying to keep our reputation as being the
No. 1 defense, and we can't do it by letting a team score on us.
The game was nothing to brag about."

At least end Wayne Hamilton, who had two sacks for a minus 20 and 11 overall tackles, was one happy Tider, telling the
press, "I think this is the best game that I've played this year, and
the best since I got hurt against USC last year."

Despite the laments in the locker room, the disappointing
game stats revealed Alabama had outgained Tech 431-178.

As far as the Homecoming festivities, Governor Fob James
crowned Cammie Williams as the Queen and former star Lee
Roy Jordan served as the Grand Marshall. Sister Sledge belted
out their song, "We Are Family" at a Thursday night concert at
Memorial Coliseum, and the official theme of the year was appropriately, "Stars Fell on Alabama."

Chapter 24

The Quarterbacks Bite the Dawgs

"You don't need to be a Phi Beta Kappa to know that Steadman [Shealy] and Don [Jacobs] won this game. I don't ever recall our quarterbacks rushing for so many yards. It couldn't happen to nicer people. Steadman is one of the best competitors we've had. You can hit him once or twice or a bunch, but sooner or later, 'It's bingo' and he's off."
—Paul Bryant

Sitting among a group of news reporters after Alabama's 24-7 victory over Mississippi State, quarterback Steadman Shealy, who had rushed for 209 yards, said, "I have a funny feeling I overcame a lot of mistakes today. I made some bad reads, then turned around and ran the ball upfield. We still lack smoothness on offense, and you can blame that on me. The quarterback is supposed to make our wishbone go."

Today, Shealy laughs about the game. "I gained all those yards and didn't grade a winner, because I wasn't making the correct reads. On one play I gained about 40 yards and got a negative because I'd misread the option. State had a great defensive team, with two great linemen in Tyrone Keys and Glen Collins. They'd make you a little quicker."

Shealy, who lost 19 yards, finishing officially with 190 yards, set a quarterback rushing record for the Tide and missed by three yards of setting the record for most yards rushing against MSU (Johnny Musso set the mark with 193 in a 40-6 win over the Dawgs in '71). Throw in the 44 net by Jacobs, and the six gained by Tommy Wilcox, and the quarterbacks combined for 240 yards rushing against MSU.

First-Half Field Position

After a scoreless first quarter, Alabama's Robbie Jones recovered a fumble on the Bulldog 30 on the first play of the second period, setting up a six-play drive. Jacobs carried the final for times, scoring from the six to make it 7-0.

With wishbone innovator Emory Bellard now coaching State, the Bulldogs appeared a mirror image of the Tide, and quarterback Dwayne Brown and his mates erased most of the time in the quarter, taking 8:23 off the clock on a drive that died on the Bama 18. Ricky Tucker broke up a pass to Mardye McDole and Randy Scott teamed with E. J. Junior to slam Brown down on the 18, forcing a field goal that sailed right.

On its only other possession of the half, the Tide was backed up after Jacobs's pitch to James Haney flew over his outstretched hands, but the Tide averted immediate trouble when Haney recovered on his own 10. After a punt by Woody Umphrey, State marched 48 yards for a tying score, with Brown hitting McDole for 20 to set up an eight-yard TD pass to tight end Jerry Price.

Third-Quarter Explosion

All the second-half scoring occurred in the third quarter, starting with a 41-yard field goal by Alan McElroy that gave the Tide a 10-7 lead with 7:12 left in the house. Shealy engineered the 72-yard drive for the three and it was his show, running for 28 and passing 30 to Keith Marks to pass 58 of those yard stripes.

On the ensuing kickoff, John Mauro dislodged the ball from Glenn Young on the 18, and four plays later Shealy darted into the end zone to up the advantage to 17-7.

As the quarter wound down, Jacobs and the second unit traveled 89 yards in nine plays for the final 24-7 margin. Billy Jackson, who had missed the Tennessee and Virginia Tech game, was back in action and made the most of his opportunity, rambling 39 yards on the first play of the drive and finishing it off on a rare screen pass that he took over the middle from Jacobs and went in untouched for a 23-yard score.

Injuries Mount

In the fourth quarter, Jacobs hobbled to the sideline with a knee injury, and Shealy, who had been nicked up pretty good and pretty winded, according to Bryant, came to the bench after starting at his 18 and flying down the field to the State 18. Third quarterback Alan Gray wasn't dressed, so Bryant inserted safety and onetime hotshot quarterback recruit Tommy Wilcox into the game as the signalcaller.

On his only carry, Wilcox netted six yards, but the drive stalled and the Tide couldn't finish it off, though the points would have been meaningless, other than to impress the ever-vacillating pollsters.

Another Record

In beating State, the Crimson Tide established yet another record—21 straight SEC victories, eclipsing the mark of 20 straight set by Tennessee under General Neyland, and it was the

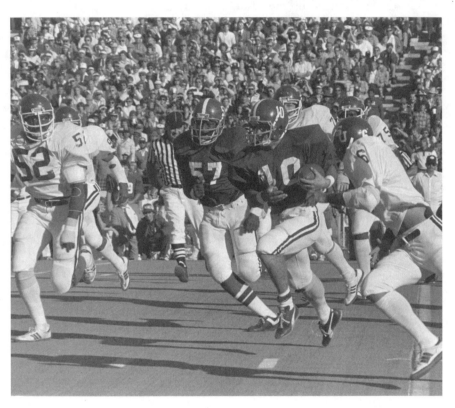

*Steadman Shealy follows a Dwight Stephenson block on a record-setting day.
(Photo courtesy of the University of Alabama Archives)*

Tide's 22nd straight over the Bulldogs—and this MSU team entered the game undefeated in the SEC and with wins over Florida and Tennessee.

Yet Bryant wasn't thinking about that mark. "I was real worried at the half. Our team showed a lot of character and class coming back they way they did. We're still injured and today didn't help. I don't know how bad Jacobs is hurt, but I don't think Shealy is too bad.

"We didn't play [defensive back] Bobby Smith today. We didn't play Jim Bob Harris in the second half, 'cause he got hurt in the first. Of course, we didn't even dress Major Ogilvie, Keith Pugh, or Alan Gray either."

Sitting in the losers' dressing quarters, puffing his ever-present pipe, Emory Bellard looked more like a professor than a coach, and in fact he was a teacher. In 1971 he had been instructed by his then boss Darrell Royal to teach the wishbone to Alabama.

"Am I sorry I taught it to Alabama?" Bellard replied to the question. "Lord, no. They've taken it and added a few characteristics, particularly in the passing game, to make it even better. The wishbone is an offense with high percentages of success, because if the quarterback properly reads the defense, the play is going to work.

"You know Alabama's personnel is really no better than ours and certainly not Tennessee's. Alabama is a great team because they are mentally tougher and they do the little things better than any of the rest of us. That man [Bryant] drills it into them that they are champions and they believe it."

Longtime *Birmingham News* sports editor Alf Van Hoose didn't disagree with Bellard's assessment, noting in a column, "Fifteen of Alabama's starters are from Alabama. One, Mike Brock, is a walk-on that nobody offered a scholarship, and eight others only got offers from Alabama. This is not unusual. It's the same most years. Coach Bryant's success can be traced directly to his coaching ability. He's the world's best coach.

"Bryant's first law is to get the best players from Alabama and most of the others from the Southeastern Conference area.

As he says, 'You better be able to develop some 'tweeners into players. They may be called suspects, but if they've guts and pride and never quit, they'll help you at some point over the next four or five years.'"

Chapter 25

A Major Surprise as Raindrops Cascaded on Tigertown

"Fellas, let me tell you one thing: Alabama is the best defensive football team I've ever seen. My gosh, what a defense."
—LSU coach Charley McClendon

The week leading up to the Alabama-LSU game was replete with anecdotes of accusatory remarks, comical quips, and the solicitation of a masseuse to try to get star halfback Major Ogilvie back into the lineup.

During that era, ABC owned the TV rights to college football, and a team could only be on five times in a two-year period. ABC, claiming it had an agreement from LSU Athletic Director Paul Dietzel to move the Tiger game to the afternoon of November 10, bypassed on the Crimson Tide's game with Tennessee.

"Absolutely, 100 percent not true," Dietzel replied to Jim Spence's allegation.

"Dietzel's 1000 percent off-base. There's no way we would have passed on the Tennessee game if we had not had assurances and commitments from LSU," said Spence, the VP of sports for the network. Regardless, the game wasn't shifted, and the bitter barbs didn't cease as the week wore on.

On a more humorous note, LSU football coach Charley McClendon—known as a king of the malapropos—held his weekly media gathering at the student union the Tuesday before the game. A Paul Bryant disciple, McClendon was in the last of his 18 years as the head coach of the Bayou Bengals, and he knew his mentor would use every psychological ploy to infuse a false sense of confidence into an opponent. Charley Mac wasn't buying into the injury theory, particularly the one to Ogilvie, whom he fully expected to play.

In reviewing the Crimson Tide personnel, Mac let fly with one of his better verbal gaffes, saying, "Alabama will have all those injured players back, especially Colonel Oliver. He's the key to their wishbone and he'll be here Saturday night."

Although McClendon may have inadvertently re-ranked the Major and called him by the wrong last name, his prognostication of Ogilvie playing seemed far-fetched in Tuscaloosa.

A Major Healing

"Let's just say I was pretty battered and bruised, and I really hadn't run any since the Tennessee game," said Ogilvie.

"I was undergoing four whirlpool treatments for 30 minutes apiece each day. Dr. Gaylon McCollough [former Tide center and then a Birmingham physician] found this Jamaican masseuse, and she was working on me, too.

"On Wednesday before the game, Joe Jones brought me the game plan, which I'm sure Coach Bryant told him to do. On Thursday, Coach asked me how I was feeling and I told him better, and he asked me to drop by practice.

"I was standing there in street clothes, and Coach Bryant wheels up in his cart and he asked me if I felt like running. I wasn't going to tell him no. Coach Goostree wrapped me up with about 10 ace bandages and I ran four or five plays.

Major Ogilvie on the run on the bayou against LSU.
(Photo courtesy of The University of Alabama Archives)

"Coach Bryant called me that night to check on me, and on Friday we worked out and I ran a few more plays. He told me he wanted me to go to Baton Rouge with the team for moral support, but I wasn't gong to dress out.

"The weather was awful. Lightning was flashing everywhere, and it was a pretty good warning of what it was going to be like in Baton Rouge. We went to Tiger Stadium for a walk-through Saturday morning, and I was surprised when I saw my equipment there. Coach told me he thought I'd be a better moral support to the team if I dressed out.

"That night we were warming up, and I was back catching punts near midfield and Coach Bryant was leaning on the goal post. Coach Goostree waddled down to me and said, 'Ogilvie, you look mighty spry tonight.'

"I told him I felt pretty good, and he waddled back to Coach Bryant and told him. He made a second trip to check on me and he waddled back to tell Coach Bryant again.

"I saw Coach Goostree coming back a third time and said, 'Old buddy, I just want to let you know Coach Bryant told me to tell you you're getting ready to start tonight.'"

McClendon's prediction had come true.

It Never Rains in Tiger Stadium?

LSU's age-old proclamation that it never rains in Tiger Stadium was drenched away this November night as the skies cried in a torrential stream of cool water, and it would have a more pronounced effect on the game than the return of the star back.

"The rain was bad enough, but we couldn't hear any of the audibles," said Ogilvie.

"Their crowd was fired up and they never quit yelling from the time we warmed up until we got out of Baton Rouge with the 3-0 win."

And, indeed, Ogilvie started the game, taking a pitch from Steadman Shealy on the Tide's first offensive play and rolling around the left side for six yards, where the Bengals' Tommy Frizzell and Willie Teal crashed him out of bounds.

"I just popped up and ran back to the huddle, feeling pretty good," said Ogilvie.

"I didn't learn until the next day that I had clipped Coach Bryant and sent him sprawling."

Ogilvie didn't hear the PA announcement either, as it boomed across Tiger Stadium, "The Major is down and so is the Bear."

Bryant didn't stay down long either, and after the game when asked about the lick, he quipped, "It's the best block Major made all night. To tell you the truth I was a heck of a lot more worried about him than me. We needed him in the lineup."

Ogilvie stayed for the entire game, which featured pools of water all over the soaked Tiger Stadium turf.

On its first series, the Tide splashed down the field to the LSU 11, but the drive stalled and Alan McElroy's 28-yard field goal sailed left.

Starting from the 50 in the second quarter, Shealy adeptly drove the Tide to the LSU 22, and on third down backup back Mitch Ferguson floated out in the flat for what appeared to be a cinch TD. Just as Shealy's pass was nearing Ferguson, he slipped on the slick soil, and the pass dropped harmlessly a few yards from him. McElroy's 39-yard field goal attempt was wide right.

LSU's lone penetration into Alabama territory occurred on the ensuing drive when quarterback Steve Ensminger broke containment at the Tiger 45 and made it to Bama's 45, where E. J. Junior tracked him down. That would be as far as the Tigers would traverse their legendary field that night.

On its first drive of the third quarter, the Crimson Tide slogged through the mud to reach the Tiger 10, where McElroy's 27-yard field goal split the uprights with 8:43 left in the third quarter. It would be the only score of the night.

"I punched the first one," said McElroy to the press after the game. "And I think the wind pushed the second one away. I was thankful for the chance at the last one. I stood on the sidelines wondering if I'd get the chance.

"On the field goal the line blocked, Barry Smith made a perfect snap and Woody Umphrey handled a wet ball to give me a perfect hold."

However, the dramatics didn't end, thanks to a decision Bryant regretted afterwards. After Mike Clements intercepted Ensminger at midfield with 6:57 left in the game, Shealy drove Bama down the field in the fourth quarter, reaching the LSU 27 with 5:25 left in the game. Facing a fourth and five, the Tide coach knew a field goal was improbable and elected to try a pass, a near-fatal mistake.

Dropping back, Shealy was trapped and sacked by LSU's John Adams at his own 40, giving the Bengals their best field position since the second quarter.

"I'd cut my throat if that stupid decision by me had cost us the game," said Bryant, knowing full well that one slip on the watery field could be disastrous.

On first down that fate almost happened as Ensminger sailed a pass toward his favorite target, Carlos Carson, who was racing past a sliding Tide secondary. Fortunately for Bama, the pass fluttered away, too far to be caught. A 10-yard completion to Hokie Gajan on the next play had the Tigers at midfield with a first down and with 4:35 to pull the upset.

This time Jim Bob Harris ensured the victory by picking off Ensminger's pass at the Alabama 40. Alabama had survived a potential watery grave on the bayou.

Postgame

With the victory secure, Alabama's Paul Bryant became the first coach ever to win 100 games in a decade, and he thanked a couple of defensive backs for saving the day. "Mike Clements and Jim Bob Harris may have made the biggest plays of our season with those interceptions."

Alabama had outrushed the Tigers 252-67, but fullback Steve Whitman came away impressed by an LSU team that had three losses by eight points to undefeated Bama, Southern Cal, and Florida State. "This is the most physical game since Penn State. Against Tennessee, we felt we could score when we needed to. But tonight, I had a lot of doubts about us winning. Any time it rains like that, it gets in your head."

For the second time, the two-month old network, ESPN, delayed-telecast the game with Jim Simpson being the play-by-play, and the comparison between the Tide and the SC Trojans was a prominent topic.

LSU's star back Gajan put it this way. "Alabama is quicker than SC and more fundamentally sound."

McClendon said, "The difference is the defense. You can't lose when the other team can't score, and that's what you face when you play Alabama."

A relieved Ricky Tucker was just happy to get out of Tiger Stadium with a win, telling the press gathering, "This is a game I'll remember all my life. It was a great win. Like Coach Goostree said, 'it was a low-scoring and a butt-swinging game.'

"It was the hardest-hitting game I've ever been in and something I can tell my grandchildren. Just beating LSU at Tiger Stadium at night is special. I don't think they've been shut out in a long time."

The next morning Ogilvie went for his whirlpool treatment when he was surprised to see Bryant in an adjacent tub getting a treatment. "I asked Coach Goostree what had happened to Coach Bryant," said Ogilive. "He told me, 'You don't know? You knocked him down pretty good on the first play.' I didn't know. I know I was scared to go back into the training room." For the record, Ogilvie graded a perfect 100 percent for his play in the storm.

Chapter 26

Meet the Redwood Forest, Jim Kelly

"John, all I can say is anyone who goes into the territory of the secondary is considered an intruder, and I can tell you one thing: they aren't treated too friendly when they get there."
—Sideline announcer Jerry Duncan to John Forney after Tommy Wilcox nearly decapitated Miami receiver Walker

For the first time ever, a football game was scheduled to be televised live from Tuscaloosa, but not because there had been any type of détente between ABC's Jim Spence and LSU AD Paul Dietzel.

"We'd never passed on the Alabama-Tennessee game if we didn't have an agreement with LSU to do their game with Alabama," spewed Spence upon announcing a network site crew had inspected Bryant-Denny and deemed it worthy of airing the contest. Dietzel didn't back down either, disputing Spence's claims.

When Paul Bryant was quizzed about the matter, he prophetically remarked, "We would never move a Tennessee game to night for TV. I think it is important to be on television, but I think they are getting way too much influence. One day they'll be telling everyone what to do and when to do it. I won't be around when it happens, but it'll happen."

Al Michaels and Frank Broyles were the announcing tandem for a game that was about as national as it could be, being listed in 85 percent of the markets across the country.

They Shalt Not Pass

Brimming with confidence, coached by former Bryant player and assistant coach Howard Schnellenberger, the Miami Hurricanes were puffing mightily after beating Penn State 26-10 in State College, as their rookie quarterback Jim Kelly completed 18 of 30 for 280 yards.

Hurricane receivers openly boasted they'd pass all over the Tide, prompting a sign to appear mysteriously in the Tide locker room, simply stating "They Shalt Not Pass."

On Tuesday before the game, Ricky Tucker told the *Tuscaloosa News'* Al Browning, "We have 20. The goal we set at the start of the year was to break the school record of 24. Yes sir, it means a lot to us. We took a lot of criticism last year and we had some points to prove and some scores to settle."

"We want them to throw the ball," Don McNeal agreed. "That gives us a challenge. We can make things happen when the ball is in the air. Once it leaves the quarterback's hands, it belongs to us just as much as it belongs to them."

And Miami did pass . . . but not very successfully. Alabama's wishbone not only outran them and outhit the 'Canes, the Tide's Steadman Shealy outshone Kelly in the air games.

"Finally having Keith [Pugh] back was the reason our passing game was so efficient," said Shealy. "Miami did everything it could to stop the run and we hit 'em in the air."

Pugh, who would be voted the ABC Player of the Game, caught a career-high seven for 133 yards. Tight end Tim Travis nabbed a 56-yarder from Shealy in the first quarter to make it 7-0 and Alan McElroy's field goal upped the lead to 10-0 at the half.

Randy Scott helped lead the defensive charge that blew away the Hurricanes. (Photo courtesy of the University of Alabama Archives)

Major Ogilvie scored on a one-yard run in the third quarter to end a six-minute drive, and McElroy's field goals of 25 and 40 made it 23-0 in the fourth. The reserves deflated the last iota of air from the Hurricanes when James Haney scored from the five late in the game for the final of 30-0.

The Secondary Welcomes Miami to Bryant-Denny

Indeed, the Hurricanes passed 28 times, to be exact, in the 51 plays they attempted. Of course, three sacks were counted as rushes as well, so Miami went back to throw 31 times.

Miami's quarterback tandem of Kelly and Mike Rodrique were rocked, knocked down and intercepted—often. In 15 attempts, the future NFL Hall of Famer Kelly completed two for 10 yards. Three of his passes were picked off.

Roderique was somewhat more successful, if you consider completing four of 13 for 37 yards and having two intercepted a good day.

Tommy Wilcox, Randy Scott, Jeremiah Castille, Al Blue and Tucker got interceptions. McNeal personally broke up four more pass attempts, one more than each of his teammates Wilcox, Tucker and Jim Bob Harris. Mike Clements added two more break ups for good measure. For the season, the Tide now had 25 interceptions, one more than the 1952, 1966 and 1968 teams. It still stands as the best ever by an Alabama team.

Kelly was left virtually speechless, murmuring this one line to the press, "It's hard for me to say anything at this moment. I didn't know where I was after I got hit in the second quarter."

Schnellenberger praised the winners. "Ken Donahue and Brother Oliver have the ability to change defenses brilliantly, and it is hard for a quarterback to figure out what they are doing. Of course, they get most of their wisdom from the big guy on the sidelines."

One Alabama player was not amused with the antics of the Miami offensive players. Defensive end E. J. Junior told the press,

"We had fun, despite their holding, the biting and the cheap shots and their big talking."

For Shealy it was his best passing day of the year, as he completed nine of 15 for 187 yards. When the defense gave him the ball, he kept the clocking churning away as the Tide held it for 40:06 on this 71-degree late November afternoon. Alabama had totaled 444 yards to Miami's 131.

"I came into this game beat up and I sure didn't get well during it," said Shealy.

"Miami did a super job of stopping the run, so we had no choice but to throw it."

If Shealy was happy to have his roommate Pugh back, he wasn't nearly as happy as the injured receiver, who told the press after the game, "This is the most passes I've caught since I had seven against Escambia Academy when I was in high school. Today, I felt good. There was some pain, but I was able to move around pretty good."

Bowl Mystery Again

Just as the 1978 bowl situation wasn't resolved until after the final weeks, the 1979 team was in an even bigger dilemma. Entering the weekend, all Georgia had to do to secure the Sugar Bowl berth was to beat Auburn, based on the last-appearance rule.

For a second straight year Auburn put a muzzle on the Bulldogs, decisively beating them 33-13 in Athens, yet an Auburn win over Alabama would still put Georgia in the Sugar and amazingly would apparently leave Alabama with nowhere to go.

Despite Bryant's request for the bowl to wait after the Alabama-Auburn game, the Cotton Bowl was already wheeling and dealing to get the loser of the Nebraska-Oklahoma game and the Orange seemed content matching unbeaten Florida State against the Big-Eight winner.

"If it is up to me, if we don't beat Auburn," said Bryant about the bowl scenario, "I'd just as soon stay home and plow."

Pugh agreed with his coach, echoing his thoughts, "If we lose to Auburn, we don't deserve a bowl bid."

Chapter 27

"Plow, Bear, Plow."

*"We knew it was a jaw-to-jaw, buckle-to-buckle
fight, and that's the kind of game Coach Bryant
loves and what he knows we love."*
—Middle guard Warren Lyles after the '79 Auburn game

Paul Bryant's statement that he'd as soon go back to plowing than go to a bowl if Alabama lost to Auburn was not lost on the Tiger student population, who chanted, "Plow, Bear, plow" when the Crimson Tide walked onto Legion Field Saturday December 1, 1979.

"Do you hear them chanting?" Charley Thornton, Bryant's TV host and longtime administrative assistant asked the coach. In apparent good pregame humor, Bryant put his arms behind in a plow-like style and let Thornton push him a few yards, eliciting momentary laughter.

But the game was going to be a knee-knocker, and Bryant knew it. Entering the game with an 8-2 overall record, Auburn's only SEC loss had come early in the season at Tennessee, and only Alabama was playing better than the Tigers in the entire Southern region.

The emotions leading up to the game were at their usual fever pitch. During an interview the week of the game, tackle David Hannah remembered "crying like a baby in 1972 when Auburn blocked the punts to win. There is no way I want to go out that way."

Steve Whitman simply said, "Beating Auburn is everything. If we lose this game, I don't want to be seen in public."

Steadman Shealy—who had appeared on the cover of the Nov. 12 *Sports Illustrated* with Nebraska's Jarvis Redwine, Ohio State's Art Schlichter, Florida State's Jimmy Jordan and Houston's Delrick Brown, with each holding up a finger designating their teams as No. 1—talked about playground football as kid in Dothan.

"We'd play Alabama vs. Auburn in the backyard. I liked both schools and I wanted to be like Pat Sullivan as a passer and Terry Davis as a runner. "I was a 13-year-old junior high school quarterback."

Offensive guard Vince Boothe said the plan would be simple. "We want to hang on to the football, control the clock, not turn it over, keep [James] Brooks and [Joe] Cribbs off the field. If we do that, we'll be all right."

Indeed, the Redwood Forest had a significant challenge in slowing down Brooks and Cribbs, the first backs in SEC history to rush for 1,000 each in a season.

The Iron Bowl

On a clear and sunny autumn afternoon, Alabama's early game frustrations served as a menacing warning of worse things to come, though one would never have deduced it by the 14-3 halftime score.

"We should have been up at least 24-3," said Shealy, noting two early failed opportunities, including the opening kickoff when Randy Scott recovered a Brooks fumble on the Auburn 23. Frank Warren sacked Shealy on a third-down pass and the Tide had to punt.

On its next series, Alabama relentlessly covered most of the yards in Legion Field, reaching the Auburn six, but Billy Jackson botched a pitch and lost 12. Alan McElroy failed on a 30-yard field goal.

Auburn converted on its first threat when Jorge Portella hit a 47-yard field goal to make it 3-0 at the end of the quarter.

Controlling the second quarter, Alabama covered 80 yards in 11 plays, scoring on a 28-yard pass from roommates Shealy and Keith Pugh. On its next series, the Tide rolled 65 yards on 10 plays, with Shealy scoring from the one with 2:53 left in the half.

A Third-Quarter Nightmare

While Alabama had given up 13 points in the second half all year, including six to Georgia Tech on last play of the game, the Alabama offense had scored 193. That figured to a 19.3-1.3 edge, so the Bama side of the field seemed confident.

Even Georgia head coach Vince Dooley, who was in the press box watching the action, conceded he didn't think his alma mater had enough to come from behind against the Tide.

Alabama would make sure the game became entertaining for the 77,918 in attendance. Five times in the third quarter Alabama fumbled. Four times Auburn recovered.

"I'll never forget the football had a dewy, moist feel to it," said Shealy. "I really can't explain why. Maybe it was because of the sun dipping over the upper deck, but it was a nightmare."

On the first play from scrimmage in the third, Shealy bobbled the ball away at his own 21, but the Redwood Forest answered the call with Hannah stopping Brooks on third down. Like Alabama had failed on its first series, the Tigers failed to score, leaving it at 14-3.

Two plays later Auburn was back in business at the Tide's 28 when Ogilvie uncharacteristically lost the ball. Byron Braggs, Hannah and Thomas Boyd stopped Cribbs's runs and forced a 39-yard field goal by Portella that sliced the lead to 14-6.

On its next play, Whitman fumbled but did recover his miscue, and ultimately the Tide at least punted out of danger. When Alabama took back over on its 28 with 7:47 left in the quarter, the Tide seemed to reassert its second-quarter dominance, moving quickly down to the Tiger 12.

Again on first down, Shealy lost the ball, and Auburn's Harris Rabren pounced on it at the 16. Auburn wasn't handling the ball much better, having already recovered one of its own bobbles in the quarter, but it was the Tide's turn to grab the elusive pigskin when Thomas Boyd's pop extricated it from the arms of Cribbs at the 22 and E. J. Junior was there to smother it for Bama.

After reaching the Tiger five, McElroy kicked a 23-yard field goal with 2:07 left in the quarter to up the lead back to 11 at 17-6. If Alabama was regaining lost momentum, it didn't last long. Usually sure-handed Wilcox botched a Skip Johnston punt at his own 36, again giving the Tigers the desired field position.

"Tommy never fumbled in practice or the games," said Shealy. "When he lost the fumble, I don't think any of us knew what to think."

Auburn took advantage with quarterback Charlie Trotman hitting Cribbs for a touchdown pass on third down from the 36, but Alabama remained ahead 17-12 when Mike Clements picked off the two-point pass attempt by Cribbs.

After the Tide's backup unit with Alan Gray in at quarterback couldn't move, Auburn momentarily took control, regaining the lead at 18-17. Wide receiver Bryon Franklin got behind the Tide secondary, and Trotman hit him for a 55-yard gain, setting up an 11-yard TD pass to Mark Robbins. Thomas Boyd stopped Trotman on the two-point try, and the Tigers were roaring.

The Drive, Part II

Did Alabama panic or momentarily lose its poise? "When Auburn took the lead, I had the greatest feeling in the world," offensive tackle Jim Bunch was quoted on the official quote page circulated by the SID staff after the game. "I knew then we had the challenge we'd been waiting for.

"I never thought about losing the game. I knew we were going to drive the ball down their throats. This was our gut check. When adversity presents itself, a champion fights back."

Starting from its 18, the drive hazardly started when Ogilvie lost control of Shealy's pitch. "I think it was the biggest play of the game," said Shealy. "By the grace of God it bounced back to Major." Ogilvie gained four on the play, moving to the 22.

Shealy ripped off gains of nine, 15 and two before hitting Pugh for a nine-yard gain. A late hit by Auburn on Pugh moved the chains to the Auburn 28. Whitman ripped through a gaping hole to the eight, and on the next play Shealy skirted off the left side for the eventual winning TD. His two-point run made it 25-18, but the fireworks were far from flashing their final light.

On the ensuing kickoff, Brooks exploded into the open field and appeared headed for a touchdown when freshman cornerback Jeremiah Castille sprinted, jumped on Brooks's back, and dragged him down on the 31.

"I knew I could catch Brooks, but catching him and tackling him are two different things," said Castille. "I knew no one else had a chance got catch him, so I just grabbed him and held on. I was scared to death."

"There wasn't any way they were going to score," said Braggs. "And they didn't."

Cribbs and Brooks took the first two rushes down to the 24 with Boyd and Scott stopping them. On third and three, freshman Wilcox crashed Cribbs down for no gain. A fourth-down pass was tipped away by Clements, stopping this drive.

After stopping the Tide, Auburn was back in Bama territory at the 37, but after Wayne Hamilton knocked Brooks down for no gain, the Tigers failed on three pass attempts. "This was the most pressure we'd been under since the Penn State game," said Hamilton in a relieved Bama dressing room.

Steadman Shealy with Coach Bryant moments before the epic drive.
(Photo courtesy of the University of Alabama Archives)

Taking over at the 37, Shealy's wishbone ran off most of the final 3:22, though Auburn had one last desperate attempt from its own nine after Umphrey's punt pinned the Tigers back.

In the locker room after the game, Shealy's excitment had hardly abated: "That was the most exciting drive of my entire career. It meant everything. I really got emotional during the drive.

"Chill bumps were going down my spine. When we were down 18-17, I said this is do or die. That was the toughest situation I'd ever been in. When we scored that was the first time I got emotional on the field. I don't think I was hot-dogging it. I was just glad we'd scored."

Defensive end Junior was equally thankful, noting, "Playing against Auburn and playing for Paul Bryant are all the incentives I need. Each player gives 110 to 120 percent, and it's not who makes the plays that matter. We are a team."

Bryant, who had been named the SEC Coach of the Year by the AP for the seventh time, said, "I've seen better games but few drives as good as the one in the fourth quarter. This team has more class on and off the field than any I've had. A loss in the Sugar Bowl won't change my mind, either. That drive in the fourth quarter convinced me of the unique qualities of this team."

The Sunday After

Bryant was in a good mood when he was shooting his TV show in Birmingham, joking with one of the station's aides, Ronnie Long, the floor manager who happened to be an Auburn fan and whom Bryant affectionately called "Shug" after his old Tiger adversary on the sidelines.

"Let's get this over, so I can go home and cry," Long said, to which Bryant said, "I wish you'd perk up. I have trouble mumbling when your state of mind is bad."

"I take a lot of crap from that man, but I love every minute of it," Long retorted. "He's a fine man, even if he's an Alabama guy. He's always called me Shug."

On Auburn coach Doug Barfield's show, he made note of the fact he thought Tommy Wilcox was overly aggressive and should have been called for some late hits.

"I just think it's funny," said Wilcox. "If the whistle hasn't blown I'm going to hit somebody. And I hadn't hit anyone after the whistle. Coach Bryant called me in his office and told me not to worry about it."

Chapter 28

The Days Leading up to the Sugar, Including a Trip to Pennsylvania

"Polls, polls, polls. I'm damned tired talking about polls."
—Paul Bryant after the Tide had dropped to No. 2

No. 2 and Trying Harder

The AP's national sports editor, Herschel Nissenson, had adopted Birmingham as his home away from home, and he tried to forewarn the Crimson Tide fans that Alabama's narrow escape against Auburn would unfairly affect the polls—and it did.

Ohio State leaped to the No. 1 spot by a one-vote margin, igniting a fury in Crimson Tide country.

"I didn't think we would drop to No. 2," said receiver Keith Pugh. "We didn't play our best game against Auburn, but I still didn't think we'd drop. It's really disappointing to be No. 1 all year and then drop out of it. I thought we showed some class coming from behind in the fourth quarter to win. We didn't play great—but we still won."

Bryant seemed more stunned by the price of a Sugar Bowl ticket with the face value being $15 each. "My gosh, I never thought I'd see a ticket cost so much," said Bryant, deflecting the talk about the polls which had Ohio State narrowly ahead of Bama with USC, Florida State, Oklahoma and Arkansas trailing.

Alabama did have a comfortable margin the UPI coaches' poll, and in the first-place votes, the Tide led 29 to 16 in the AP voting.

One of Arkansas's coaches was John Mitchell, the first African-American captain and All-American at Alabama, and the Razorback staff had visited the Alabama defensive coaches in the spring. "My experience as a player at Alabama gives me a base on what they like to do," said Mitchell, entertaining reporters. "Will that trip come back to haunt Alabama? I certainly hope so."

The Trip to Bridgeport

On December 19, 1979, Paul Bryant braved a snow and sleet storm in the Northeast to fulfill his commitment to speak in Pennsylvania to the Bridgeport Booster Club.

"I got up that morning, six days before Christmas, and it was snow and ice everywhere," said Johnny Nicola, the president of an organization in the unlikeliest of territories, a truck stop town 17 miles from Philadelphia "I was on the phone with Coach Bryant and he said he'd be there. When he told you something, you could bet on it. Bridgeport was like a skating rink, there was so much ice on the road."

Bryant had told Nicola the previous spring that he was going to speak to his group, which even caught the optimistic booster by surprise. With 500 tickets rapidly sold and with other speakers such as Mel Allen and Richard Todd coming down from New York, Nicola had pulled off a feat deemed impossible. "Somebody said it would be comparable to getting the Pope to speak at our church," said Nicola. "It was that big."

*Bridgeport booster Johnny Nicola introduces Coach Bryant in
the biggest day in the history of the Pennsylvania town.
(Photo courtesy of Paul Bryant Museum)*

Then the snows came, and Allen and Todd never got past the big city to get to Philadelphia and neighboring Bridgeport. Bryant, along with Aruns Callery of the Sugar Bowl, Birmingham entertainer Bob Cain, and former assistant Dude Hennessey, boarded a private plane and headed into the worst of storms. "It was the worst flight I was ever on," said Callery, "but we made it."

Nicola had coaxed the Pennsylvania state police to escort the visitors the 20 or so miles to Bridgeport. "I told Coach Bryant that Mel Allen couldn't make it, and he just said, 'Heck, Mel would have talked too long anyway.'

"Coach Bryant talked for 50 minutes and never mentioned football. You could have heard a pin drop when he spoke. He had given me a houndstooth hat a few years before and we had it bronzed for him. He stayed and autographed every last item people put in front of him.

"We've had a lot of other coaches and presidents from the University come speak to our club, but there was never a moment like the day Coach Bryant came to town. It was the biggest moment in the history of Bridgeport. No one can tell you what No. 2 is."

The Bridgeport group became intrigued with the Crimson Tide when their native son Tony Chiccino played for Bryant at Kentucky and with Hennessey, and they soon adopted Tuscaloosa as their home away from home. In 1970, Nicola and 23 others started the club, which included a bylaw stating that when the Tide wins a national championship, a billboard goes up on Route 202.

"We caught a lot of flack after the Penn State game in '79 because of the billboard," said Nicola. "There was even a national AP photo of it. We weren't trying to offend Penn State. We were just supporting Coach Bryant and the Crimson Tide."

The club is still alive and well, Nicola still presides over his coterie of Crimson friends near Philly, and they annually make at least one trip to Tuscaloosa for a game and to deliver to the University a check for their endowment for a student from their area who attends UA.

Yet Nicola still pines for the days of Bryant, reverently saying, "As far as I'm concerned, Coach Bryant is the greatest man
ever to set foot on the soil of Alabama. You can take all the lead-
ers from the state and put them with all the coaches of all the
sports from every school, and combined they wouldn't be half
the man Coach Bryant was."

Players and the Coach Reflect

On the eve of the game, three seniors considered their careers and accomplishments at Alabama.

This team is a lot looser than last year," said corner Don
McNeal. "It has to do with Gary DeNiro and Byron Braggs. They
do their 'All is Fine in 1979 Show' and they have everyone in
stitches. They keep everyone loose with their jokes. This team
simply never panics or gets upset. Even in the Auburn game when
we got behind 25-18, no one panicked."

"I love pressure games," simply said Wayne Hamilton. "They
make me play better. I wish I hadn't been hurt against SC last
year 'cause I think I could have made the difference."

"My freshman year was awful," remembered Shealy. "I came
and was the No. 8 quarterback. I thought about quitting. I prayed
about it, stayed and things changed drastically. I stayed after practice in the spring, just like in high school. I got screamed at,
chewed out, gnawed on, but I immediately saw it helping me.
The experience made me realize nothing in life comes without a
price."

Paul Bryant had almost gone to his home state school out of
high school, but he followed his heart and Don Hutson to Alabama. He came a lot closer to being the Arkansas coach.

"On a Sunday morning in 1941, I loaded up in a car with
Bill Dickey, the great New York Yankee catcher, and headed to
Arkansas to meet the governor," said Bryant, then an assistant
coach at Vanderbilt, told Van Hoose. "The deal was already pretty
much set up for me to be the next coach at Arkansas. When we

crossed the Tennessee-Arkansas state line, we heard on the radio about Pearl Harbor. We just turned around and headed back to Nashville. We never said another word the entire way home."

Glib junior lineman Byron Braggs wanted to talk about his coach, instead of the fluent Holtz. "Coach Bryant is a good man with his words. He may not be flowering like Lou Holtz, but when you use words like Coach Bryant, an intellectual vocabulary is not needed. The man is a magician when it comes to getting a team ready to play."

Sugar Bowl Pix Op

A young 14-year-old coyishly ambled up to Coach Bryant during a Sugar Bowl photo opportunity and asked to have his picture taken with him. The teenager was Kevin Holtz, the son of the Arkansas coach.

"It was bad enough my players wanted to have their pictures taken with Coach Bryant, but I didn't want to tell them that I wanted to have my taken with him as well," said Coach Holtz, who continued by talking about Alabama defensive end E .J. Junior. "No one can block E. K. Junior. I don't have a plan to slow him down."

Bryant responded, "As smart and as brilliant as you are, Lou, I'd think you'd learn his name is E. J. I'm going back to the hotel and tell him you called him E. K."

"That's all right, I'll just call him sir all night," laughed Holtz.

Last Hurrah for the Hannah Family

Senior defensive tackle David Hannah was the last of a legacy of Hannahs who had starred at Alabama, starting with his father Herb and uncle Bill. His brothers John and Charley had left the Capstone for NFL stardom, causing the youngest Hannah, who had fought back from two knee operations to earn All-SEC honors, to say, "I always wanted to play for Alabama. Dad always went to the Alabama games, but when it came time to pick, he was the most liberal. Go to the place that makes you the happiest. That place was Alabama." Collectively the Hannahs would be 125-25-4 during their Alabama careers, and David would have the distinction of being the one who played on a perfect team.

Chapter 29

Sugar Sweet Pork Roast

"I don't see how in the world anyone in the nation
could beat this team. My word, what a team."
—Arkansas coach Lou Holtz after the 1980 Sugar Bowl

"When Coach Bryant read the Arkansas scouting report to the team, he said, 'They've got a great, young, smart coach,'" remembered Mal Moore, the offensive coordinator of the Tide. "After a pause and with everyone's attention, he finished, 'I love going against smart coaches.' The players loved it, and I think right then and there we had the game won."

For what was supposed to be a sweet afternoon, it did start rather sour for the Tide when Don McNeal fumbled the opening kickoff at the Arkansas 25, but the Razorbacks were forced to try a field goal and Ish Ordonez gave the Hogs an early 3-0 lead.

It wouldn't last long, as Shealy steered the "new look double wing offense" 82 yards in seven plays with Major Ogilvie scoring on a 22-yard sprint down the left side of the Hog defense.

"I think the Sugar Bowl was Coach Moore's finest moment," said Shealy. "We put in the double wing to confuse Arkansas and we did. It was the same wishbone plays with a new look, and it caught them off guard."

Arkansas quarterback Kevin Scanlon was having a difficult time dealing with the intense pressure from the ends E. J. Junior and Wayne Hamilton, and after a Hamilton sack, Scanlon botched a snap at his own 24 with 4:59 left in the first quarter. Four plays later Ogilvie was over the top for a 14-3 lead.

The Quick Kick

"We were practicing in Tuscaloosa on Christmas Day when Coach Bryant told Joe Jones and me to stay after practice," said Ogilvie.

"He put in the quick kick that day. I'd kicked some in high school and I think the quick kicks made Coach Bryant about as happy as anything else in the game."

"The only plays I called all day were the quick kicks," said Bryant after the game. "For years, the quick kick was our best play. I've been threatening all year to put it back in and didn't. This week we put it in. We didn't work on it for more than five minutes, but it worked."

After pinning the Tide back on its one in the second quarter, Ogilvie took a pitch from Shealy and booted a 43-yarder to push Arkansas back near midfield. Alabama would eventually regain field position when the Major ran an Arkansas punt back 50 yards to the Pigs' 30 and with :25 left in the half, Alan McElroy connected on a 25-yard field goal to make it 17-3.

Arkansas made it a game in the third, traveling 80 yards on the opening drive and scoring on a fourth-and-three pass from Scanlon to Robert Farrell. Thomas Boyd and Hamilton sacked Scanlon on a two-point try to leave it at 17-9.

Then, it was Joe Jones's time to quick kick after a clip negated a first-down try for Bama, and Jones hit a 40-yarder to push Auburn back to its own 40. Tommy Wilcox, playing in his native city, broke up two passes and teamed with E. J. Junior for a third- down stop to slow down the Razorbacks.

The Drive: Part III

Early in the fourth quarter, backed up on its own two and with the Razorbacks enraged, it was time for a drive. Like Jeff Rutledge had operated against Nebraska in '78 and how Shealy had performed against Auburn four weeks earlier, the Alabama offense would begin a relentless attack that would deliver national championship results.

"Teams may shut us down once or twice, but sooner or later as Coach would say, 'It is bingo,'" said Shealy, talking about the drive. On first down Whitman powered ahead for six and then Ogilvie battered ahead for seven to the 15 before throwing a key block on Billy Jackson's 35-yard blast to midfield. A play later Jackson got 14 more and then it was Ogilvie for three.

Shealy kept it for 22 to the 11 and Whitman finished it with an 11-yard run up the middle for the 24-9 lead.

"It was a 43-read and even before I hit the line, I knew it was the big one," Whitman. "Arkansas was probably expecting us to go outside. They changed their defense at the last second and took Steadman instead of me. I saw the goal line at the three and I knew we needed it. I just muscled into the end zone from there."

Arkansas's safety Keith Evans felt the brunt of the final surge by Whitman being bowled over at the three.

After a Wilcox interception, Alabama misfired on one last scoring attempt. "I had Keith [Pugh] wide open for a touchdown," said Shealy. "My adrenaline was really flowing and I overthrew him. He still reminds me about it every time I see him. I don't know if he's every forgiven me for that one."

Jim Bob Harris intercepted Scanlon in the waning seconds, giving the Tide two for the day, but back then the bowl stats didn't count on the official total.

The MVP and Mrs. Bryant

For the first time the Sugar Bowl used a panel of 24 writers and broadcast journalists to select the MVP of the game. Ogilvie won the Miller-Digby Trophy by receiving 10.5 votes to edge Jackson, who had 10. Shealy had garnered three votes while Wayne Hamilton had netted one full ballot plus splitting the one with Ogilvie.

In accepting the award, Ogilvie expressed more concern about Mary Harmon Bryant than he did about earning a trophy.

"We were sitting in Coach Bryant's suite, Mrs. Bryant and me, and she was really sick," said Ruby Kassouf, who had been asked to skip the game and serve as a nurse to the coach's wife. "I know she was happy about winning the game but more happy when Major talked about how the players were thinking about her."

Obviously, concerned about his wife, Paul Bryant made a quick exit from the stadium, saying he was going back to the Fairmont to watch the Rose Bowl and check on his wife.

The players were in a convivial mood, tossing coaches in the showers, perhaps a precursor to the Gatorade baths of the future, though defensive brain Ken Donahue almost escaped. "He was almost out of there when Warren Lyles caught him, tossed him over his shoulder and tossed him in," said Jeff Rouzie, the linebacker coach.

In a spontaneous salute, the players presented the game ball to secondary mentor Bill "Brother" Oliver, who had accepted the head job at UT-Chattanooga and was coaching his final game under Bryant.

The T-Shirt

On the morning of January 2, Ruby Kassouf, who had sat with Mrs. Bryant during the game and had been in charge of the

Bryant gets his final national championship victory ride.
(Photo courtesy of the University of Alabama Archives)

Alabama hospitality suite, caught the elevator to make one final visit to the Coach and his wife.

"I was with Aruns [Callery] and Debby Jones from the Sugar Bowl, and we were going to look at the trophy," said Kassouf. "Billy Varner let us into the suite and Coach was sitting at a table with a brand new T-shirt and blue pants on. I'll never forget it. I said, 'Coach Bryant, do you realize you have a tear in your shirt?'

"He said, 'Ruby, I always make a tear in my t-shirts, so I'll never forget where I came from.' He told me he never had a new shirt when he was a child growing up in Arkansas and he wasn't going to forget his roots."

There wasn't much concern this time around about the polls. Southern Cal had beaten Ohio State in the Rose Bowl, ensuring the Crimson Tide would be the lone perfect team. By the time the Crimson Tide had made it back to Tuscaloosa to celebrate, the proclamations of No. 1 were already ringing in another new year.

Chapter 30

The Aftermath of Being No. 1

"The only feeling better than playing for the national title in the Sugar Bowl on January 1 is being in Tuscaloosa on January 2 to celebrate after you've won it."
—Byron Braggs after the Tide's national title coronation

"Could we compete with teams of the day?" asks big Byron Braggs. "Let's put it this way, if my teammates and myself saw the big man in the houndstooth hat leaning on a goal post, staring down the field at his team, we'd suit up today.

"Who's supposed to be the best in the SEC? Tennessee or Auburn. Well, if the big man were the sidelines, we'd take 'em on, play 'em in a doubleheader and send them both home with a whipping.

"We were a team, a real team."

"I think the thing that separated the 1978 and 1979 teams from the others I coached and played on was the football IQs of those teams," said Rouzie, also a key component in molding the revered 1992 Crimson Tide defense. "We had dedicated players, totally committed to Coach Bryant's philosophy and they learned what we taught them quickly. Those were exceptional teams and

I was fortunate to coach some great linebackers during a special time at a special place."

"People ask me all the time which defense was better, the one in 1979 or the one we had in '92," added Bill Oliver, who along with Rowzie helped coach both of them. "Let's just put it this way, I don't think there were many offenses then or now that would want to have much to do with either one of them. I'll leave the debates to some media experts."

The Fifth AP Title and Shealy's Honors

When the final polls were released, Alabama had clinched its fifth Associated Press title for Paul Bryant, one more than Notre Dame's Frank Leahy and two more than Minnesota's Bernie Bierman and the Oklahoma duo of Bud Wilkinson and Barry Switzer.

Southern California was second in the final polls ahead of Oklahoma, Ohio State, Houston, Florida State, Pittsburgh, Arkansas, Nebraska and Purdue.

Quarterback Steadman Shealy had been honored as an NCAA "Top Five and Silver Anniversary Award" winner. He had also earned a National Football Foundation and Hall of Fame Scholarship.

North Carolina State's Jim Richter won the Outland Trophy, signifying him as the nation's best lineman. Dwight Stephenson had to settle for the Jacobs Trophy as the SEC's best blocker and a Hall of Fame career with the Miami Dolphins. Stephenson did make the *Football News'* All-American team while Jim Bunch was an AP, Coaches and Football Writer's All-American. Don McNeal settled for the NEA and *Sporting News* teams.

Besides Stephenson, Bunch and McNeal, Crimson Tide stars Shealy, Mike Brock, Major Ogilvie, E. J. Junior, David Hannah, Jim Bob Harris and Thomas Boyd earned first-team All-SEC honors. Tommy Wilcox was the Freshman of the Year. Wayne Hamilton, Byron Braggs and Steve Whitman were on the second team.

Big Byron Braggs did some celebrating during his Bama days.
(Photo courtesy of the University of Alabama Archives)

A Record That Still Stands

For the 1979 season, Alabama averaged 428.6 yards a game, while the defense yielded 180.1 for a 248.5 differential, the best in the history of the Southeastern Conference. The closest anyone would come to matching it would be Florida's 1996 national championship that average 503.9 on offense but gave up 281.1 on defense for a 222.8 difference.

Alabama controlled the ball nearly 36 minutes per game during that season, outscored its opponents 359-58, had 18 different players rush the ball as well as score points, six different ones attempt a pass, 14 different ones intercept a pass, 18 different ones break up at least one pass, 10 different ones recover at least a fumble.

Auburn's 249 total offensive yards were the most on the team for the entire season, and that was three less yards than Bama rushed for against LSU in the rainstorm in Baton Rouge.

Epilogue

The official Sugar Bowl scoreboard lights flashed with the final score of Alabama 14, Penn State 7 while at the same time wishing everyone a Happy New Year. According to a digital timer it was 4:03 p.m., January 1, 1979.

ABC-TV announcer Keith Jackson joined old friend Aruns Callery, who knew the location of a hidden service elevator where they could escape the masses that were exiting the Superdome. Dr. H. Boyd McWhorter, the commissioner of the Southeastern Conference, and I were meandering through a maze of people trying to find our own escape route when we met up with Callery and Jackson. Forever the gentleman, Callery asked us to join his private parade.

Boarding the concealed elevator, we started our descent to the basement of the superstructure.

"Men, you've just witnessed a classic," said Jackson. No other words needed to be spoken, and I don't think there were.

Commissioner McWhorter wanted to see Paul Bryant and extend his congratulations, and Callery directed us through a series of alleyways to the back door of a dimly-lit interview room, where an ABC television camera haloed a yellowish light around sideline announcer Jim Lampley, who was interviewing the MVP of the game, Barry Krauss.

Standing in a corner with his PR man Charley Thornton, having already been interviewed or waiting to be interviewed, Bryant nodded at our entry.

The SEC's best-ever coach and the conference's best-ever commissioner, both old navy veterans of more important battles, clasped hands. Dr. McWhorter, equally eloquent in quoting Biblical scriptures or Shakespeare, simply said, "Paul, that's the damndest sequence of defensive plays I've ever seen. Gosh amighty, I've never seen anything like it."

Without a hint of braggadocio, the old coach proudly uttered, "There's only one team that could have made those plays, and that team is Alabama."

After sharing a few thoughts, the coach headed to the podium to meet the press, while the commissioner sought us out to the exit the area and leave the coach and his players to their special moment. Turning around, we watched the old warrior on the podium, mumbling in his best gravel pitch, "There was only one team that could have stopped Penn State on the goal line and that team was Alabama." Pausing and peering through the TV lights with squinted eyes, he simply said, "It was a time of champions."